# taking note

## a year at home with strangers

# taking note

## a year at home with strangers

### bill elkington

Llumina Christian Books

ISBN: 1-932560-76-9

Printed int the United States of America by Llumina Christian Books

For Pat

"The books the Holy Spirit is writing are living, and every soul a volume in which the divine author makes a true revelation of his word, explaining it to every heart, unfolding it in every moment."

Jean-Pierre de Caussade
*The Sacrament of the Present Moment*

"That which was from the beginning, which we have heard, which we have seen with our eyes, which we have looked at and our hands have touched—this we proclaim concerning the Word of life. The life appeared; we have seen it and testify to it, and we proclaim to you the eternal life, which was with the Father and has appeared to us. We proclaim to you what we have seen and heard, so that you also may have fellowship with us. And our fellowship is with the Father and with his Son, Jesus Christ. We write this to make our joy complete."

1 John 1:1–4

# Table of Contents

# Acknowledgements

I want to thank the members of my church (you know who you are) who appear spiritually if not bodily and by name throughout the book. I want to thank the stars of my Home Fellowship, who appear as chapter headings in the Table of Contents. I am particularly grateful to Jim and Elaine for opening their home to me. I want to thank Billy and Minnie for hovering over me.

Finally, Ken has provided the persistent encouragement that I seem to have needed to shove this book out the door. And so I thank him. I think.

# Introduction

ome Fellowship. Sounds cozy, doesn't it? But what is it? I wondered, when Elaine first invited me to hers, shortly after I became a Christian. What do they do there? Is any of it illegal? Any of it weird? Do people act like characters in the *Twilight Zone*, for example? Like characters in the Moony satires on the old *Saturday Night Live*?

Why do they do it, have it? Is there any idol-worship involved? Must one own a pair of plastic praying hands? Hang a cross from one's rear view mirror? Why isn't church enough? Isn't sitting around with a lot of Christians all evening going to be, well, kind of odd? Aren't Christians, in general, kind of odd? The ones who've gone off the deep end? Who talk about God a lot? Who pray out loud? Who read the Bible because they actually like it?

It took awhile before my palms weren't sweaty anymore. Before I actually opened up my mouth and said something. Anything.

My hosts—Elaine and Jim—and the rest of the group, including transients, were scary at first, the way a family is scary to a newly-adopted son or brother. He's on the outs until he's not, and who knows how long that will be, in the beginning? Forever, maybe, is what one thinks. What the new boy thinks.

But turns out it wasn't a horror show after all. Wasn't a long ordeal involving a lot of strange family politics. No cultic rituals. No blood sacrifices. No snakes.

Just a bunch of folks who worshipped, and prayed, and studied, and read, and laughed, and ate, and chatted, and joked, and cried, and discovered things together. A collection of Christians come together to be Christians with one another. Out of church. In the world. With only God there to help.

The idea for the book came to me as I got to know these people, began to discover how extraordinary these ordinary people were, how deserving of others' notice.

The organization is alphabetical. By name. Because what I want to give you is these individual people I've come to know, what they're like: what God's like in them

14

and what they're like in God. And I have no better way to order them.

I mean this to be like a group of snapshots or stills with brief notes written in pencil on the back of each one to provide the context. To give you a feeling for what was going on when the image was made. What to look for as you scan the faces.

The form I've chosen is static—the form of the photograph—with dynamism implicit.

And the form is inconclusive. A photograph doesn't move toward an end. It's simply there, as most of life is there, when one slices it into its individual frames. It's individual moments.

And that's what I want to point to here. The individual moments. And what it feels like to live in them. Because that's mostly what we have after all: moment after moment.

In addition, this form seemed to want a style that would go with it. Hence the fragments. The notational, tentative, rushed, unresolved feeling of the prose itself. The style of one's thoughts as one moves from moment to moment and regards those moments.

As to the accuracy, a couple of comments. There were a few people who asked for changes to their stories to bring them right with the facts and to provide a proportionate emphasis. And I made those few changes here and there.

Others grumbled a little, including Billy, who said, "I'm kind of gruff." I asked Minnie (Billy's wife) about that. What she said was, "You see what you see." But then later Billy reread it and said, "It's okay."

You see what you see. What a remarkable thing to have said.

Elaine wanted me to picture her more like Ed— smarter is what she said she wanted, laughing. When I asked Jim (Elaine's husband) about this, he said, "She is what she is. She can't be like Ed. None of us can."

Elaine also said, "In some places I just laughed right out loud. I couldn't help it."

Barclay declared it "fine." And so did Tori. And so did Jim.

My wife, Pat, didn't like the way it ended. "Maybe?" she asked. "What kind of ending is that?"

Anne Marie was so complimentary about the thing, I've been embarrassed with her ever since.

Susan declared it, "wonderful, with reservations." And then about her chapter in particular, she said, "I ought to wring your neck."

My sister, Nancy, pointed out several errors, one of which was that she has been a Christian for a great long time, while I had written she was not. Not at all.

Ken was embarrassed about how good he came out. I offered to rough him up a bit, but he declined.

Three people asked to be removed altogether. It was a difficult time in their lives, and they didn't want their intense unhappiness during that period there staring at them for the rest of their lives.

Two asked me to change their names for confidentiality. I did. I changed other names because either I couldn't track the people down, or I thought getting permission to use their names would prove impossible or too painful for them. I also changed names of people who are only mentioned in passing. I expect they wouldn't have minded being included in the book, but I wasn't patient enough to submit the manuscript to them for their approvals.

Of the twenty names in the chapter titles, I changed five. And I fictionalized some of the material in non-essential ways to preserve people's confidentiality.

The period covered is a little over a year: from September of 2000 to December of 2001.

This is what a Home Fellowship is like, what it can be like. Who to expect. How it works. What it feels like. To somebody like me, anyway. Maybe to somebody like you.

It's about people I've come to care for. How they behave and think. What they do and say. How they carry their faith about with them.

It's about other things as well, I think. But you'll be the judge of that.

Bill Elkington
June 2003

# Anne Marie

Thirty or so. Long brown hair. Native Floridian. A slight southern richness in the way her voice moves through each particular word and between the words. Bohemian restaurant owner with her husband Michael. Biology major who spent a year or so in the field after graduation. And that's it. Then worked putting together camping trips, retreats, activities for young women over a period of years. Now working at the restaurant and at making a baby.

Came to the Home Fellowship a few years ago single. Jim and Elaine, the Home Fellowship leaders and sponsors, in whose home we meet and in whose hearts we reside, helped her move. No family. No friends in the area. Life savers, she says. Before she meets Michael.

Past year or so, she hasn't attended the church the rest of us attend. Says she couldn't in good conscience under our minister's authority. Says she has tried a dozen other churches and hasn't found more genuine, Spirit-filled praise and worship. Better gospel teaching.

Prays like this: "Yeshua, we lift Billy up to You for healing. We pray that You cleanse the arteries of his heart of the deposits that are in them and that You increase the blood supply to his heart so that he may regain the vigor of his youth. We pray that You heal him and perfect him in every way, in his arteries and his cardiovascular system as a whole, and in every other part of his body that may be experiencing problems. We pray also, if it is pleasing to You, that You work in his body to prevent future disease from lodging there; that You keep his arteries clean and healthy. We ask these things in Your name."

Restaurant doubles as an antique store. An antique hoard. Chandeliers, old plates, pictures, sculpture, wine racks, and radiators. Vases, bowls, lamps, bric-a-brac, boxes, old trays. An interior darkness opened by blades of Florida window light. Narrow sidewalk seating out front. Granite topped tables. Wrought iron chairs. Big, thick slabs of granite cut out of something larger, something architectural perhaps, and imported to this use. Display cases. In the middle, a bar.

Train tracks out back. Just out back. When a train rolls through, its horn going, one almost thinks it's traveling directly over the top of one's table.

In contrast, the serving people are young. College age. Not too many pins stuck through lips and tongues and eyebrows and weird places in the ears. Some. Enough to notice. Not enough to make one cringe. Actors. Models. Artists. Writers. Musicians. Fresh as water out of a spring in deep north woods. Open as Iowa sunflowers in August.

Menus tilted toward the immortals. Those who are confident in their immortality. Full of delicious cheeses and eggs, sweet full things like cheese lasagna and spinach lasagna, quiche, mozzarella brioche, spinach and ricotta brioche.

Home's a one story calmness. Pool in the back. Open. No screen. A real pool. A pool of a reputable size. None of these half measures taken in modern Florida homes. A pool one might actually swim in, not merely wade placidly about in like a geriatric case. Antiques again. Much wood. Ark dark wood. Flowers out front. Fountain of brash color. A celebration.

House blessing is a crowded business. Home Fellowship people. Church people. Artist and writer and actor and musician people. Elbow to elbow, knee to knee. House full.

Barclay, the retired pastor, leading Michael and Anne Marie from room to room. Dipping the long-stemmed rose like a wand in the holy water Anne Marie carries like the Holy Spirit itself in her two hands, dousing the house everywhere with the sacramental liquid. Uttering the blessing words out of the paper he holds and we hold also, following where we can. Bedrooms, bathrooms, living room, dining room, entry, kitchen. Down the narrow hallway and back.

Then it is the Eucharist in the kitchen, all of us circled there. First, prayer, holding hands together. Then the bread and the wine passing hand over hand, administered by each of us in turn to the other, counter-clockwise, eyes widening as we say, "The body of Christ, the bread of heaven" and "The blood of Christ, the cup of salvation."

So the blessing made and the communion given and taken, we line up for salad and venison and cheese ravioli and desserts and drinks and a lively conversation one with the other into the night until one by one and two by two we take our leave well-satisfied and refreshed and imbued and held. Impressed upon one's memory—Barclay's careful dousing, the holy water glistening the house, lightening us and the spaces between us. How enormous it must be to live in a house that has been blessed like this.

At the beginning of my time in the Home Fellowship— second night maybe—after the group stops for dinner and the rest migrate into the kitchen, Anne Marie says, "I've been in situations where I didn't know anyone, really, and I sat there quiet, like you, hoping no one would notice me."

"I know what you mean," I reply, coloring a little, I think, sudden heat on my face.

"So how long have you been attending this Home Fellowship?"

"Five years. No, six. Maybe seven. Something like that. I was single when I started. The people here really helped me through some tough times. Especially Jim and Elaine."

"They seem super."

"Yes, they are."

Jim sells me a ticket to a fund raising event for a local charity. It is music and standup at a local, private art gallery. Eighty or a hundred people show up. Jim and Elaine are there. Kirsten, their red-headed daughter, with her red-headed son, Geoffrey. Kirsten with the ever-present smile she's learned from her white-haired father and her red-haired mother.

After initially speaking with Jim, Elaine, Kirsten, and Geoffrey, I wander around, looking at the prints and sculptures and paintings, listening to the music and standup, etc. Get tired of the wandering. Take up a position against a corner in the railing on the ramp leading into the court-yard in the back where most of the people are and where the music and standup are being performed.

Anne Marie appears about the time I figure it's time to go. She walks over. Parks herself next to me, back in the railing's turning I've claimed and gets out of me when I plan to move my wife and children down, what the kids are up to, what my wife, Pat, is in general doing, and so forth. Talks about her work before Michael, the long spiritual draught because her work kept her uninvolved with church. About the restaurant. The ins and outs. I've always thought I'd enjoy owning and operating a res-taurant, I say. Seems like it would be a rewarding thing, pleasing people that way.

"A lot of work. A lot of hours," she says. "But we like it. We're grateful."

One feels cared for. Fussed over. Drawn out. One feels deeply grateful oneself. The alternative being one's rather empty apartment and the enforced society of oneself.

I'm not sure how the monks do it. Keep to themselves. Without being crushed under the weight of themselves. One wants to be brought out of oneself and into others. Out of one's rather grim and maculate self.

And through them into God. This seems natural. The other would seem to require much more courage or self-discipline or heavy lifting or something. I don't doubt people are made that way or that God leads them that way. For oneself, however, one has one's doubts.

At the Home Fellowship Christmas party, Anne Marie tells me she has witnessed to the people at her restaurant recently, her employees. "I was reluctant," she said. "I didn't want to seem to coerce anyone. On the other hand, I feel a responsibility to say what I believe. You never know whose life you'll touch.

"I gathered them together one day and spelled it out for them. Just told them straight out about Jesus and the life in the Spirit. About the joy one finds in Him. Nobody seemed to mind. A couple of them have approached me to learn more. We'll see where it leads. I'll probably do it again."

One night, she brings her mother to Home Fellowship. Trained in mathematics. Works for the Air Force most of her career. When Anne Marie was a girl, her teacher asked her what her mother did at work, but she wasn't sure. So she asked. Turned out her mother was responsible for mathematical analysis of airstrip designs, to determine their vulnerability to various kinds of attacks. Now she's doing Air Force strategic planning. She explains what this is about. Anne Marie sits there, lovely, strutting among us, chin in the air, her smile on parade. Showing off her mom.

And one night she brings in a frog to show us. "F-R-O-G," she says. "Reminds me of something I need to know. Funny way to do it."

Stuffed. Green. Cute in the way stuffed animals are cute. (A cuteness one is assumed to like.) "Fully Rely On God," she says. "Been struggling with what He wants from me. What He's asking me to do.

"I look at the frog here, and then I'm reminded. Recollected. 'Ok, then,' I say. 'Well, let's have it. Show me the way.'"

And then I take that away also and visit home. Visit my children and wife in Indiana. Discover Nate's been given a gift. A scholarship from a college. Their best academic scholarship. How they figure he has the grades, I'll always wonder about.

It's a gift. They translate his 12-point-scale average into a 4-point-scale average. He has a 9.6. I divide by three. That gives him a 3.2. Well under the 3.6 required.

I call the admissions guy. "We got this letter. I'm confused. Must be some mistake," I say. "He doesn't qualify."

"I'll look," he said. Minute later, he says, "No. He does qualify. We translated his grades into a 3.725."

"Oh," I say. "Thanks." Mystical arithmetic. God's hand, fudging the numbers.

Well, there are accelerated this and that in there. Advanced placement this and that. But still.

Senior year, which they don't have grades for, he's been majoring in video games and the History Channel. Hanging with his friends. Grades go into the blender. Drives his mother up one side of the water tower and down the other. I peel her off the crockery more than once.

Then comes the possibility of the gift. Invitation to compete for the gift. Some interviews. Meet the faculty. Nate and Pat fly down. Then the phone call comes. Then the letter. Their best gift. All for him.

And now, Sunday, getting ready to get back on the plane for Florida, I'm sitting beside Nate. On his bed. Tears streaming. Nose snuffling. Quiet now after all the screaming between him and his mother about how he isn't studying. And how she has turned his life into a prison. A hell. With all her nagging. All she wants to talk about is what a lousy job he's doing. About the scholarship. All it is is money, after all.

And now he says his pastor, his youth pastor, all his friends. All they want to talk about is this scholarship. How he better make sure his grades are good enough. How he'd better not blow it. How this is big. How this is important. How he'd better this and that. Blubbering.

And then I introduce frogs into the conversation. Frog on the edge of the coffee cup I use that morning. Stuffed animals. Cute. Silly, really. How Anne Marie has told me about frogs. Showed me hers. Green and fuzzy. Did I say fuzzy. How I've recently received an education on them.

How the important thing isn't what I say or his mom says or this pastor says or his friends say. How he needs to figure out what God says. And then do that.

Just rely on that. Do what He says. Do it as well as he can. And then let it go. Let it go to God. Then it will be okay.

Ask Him. Not me. Not Mom. Not his friends. Not his pastor.

Tears stop. Calm. We hug. I leave.

What an enormous gift. This business about frogs. Just like that. Easy as that. Sudden wormhole out of humanness and into God. Or froghole, maybe I should say.

Home Fellowship. Asks for prayers for her fertility. She and Michael would like a child, and they have been trying for some time. Trying to make it happen. But it hasn't. Gone to the doctors and gone through the tests, and it's her. The biology major. And so this is all fascinating. Intensely interesting. But of course frustrating as well, since the objective isn't so much a biology lesson as a child. And now, well, the various approaches are not working and the doctor has recommended moving on to the next level. Next level of fertility drug. And this drug results 50% or 60% of the time in multiples. In twos or threes or even fours or fives. And this is not something Anne Marie fancies. Trying to carry two or three or four or five children all at once. Or to raise them. She'd like one. One at a time. The old fashioned way. "Pray for guidance," she asks.

Also she asks prayer for guidance on the sale of the restaurant. The antique-shop-restaurant-coffee-house establishment she and Michael have poured their lives into for years. A buyer—a couple—has offered full price or what she and Michael consider full price for the business, and now it is a matter of the terms and conditions. And they are going back and forth. And she doesn't know what is right or wrong, and so she has placed this decision in God's hands and wants His guidance. Michael is tired and wants to sell. He has dealt with the same problems over and over. Parking. Employees and their inconsistencies. Taxes. Food. Other business owners in the area and their suspiciousness, their lack of cooperation. He put the business out there a year ago, but nothing satisfactory has come along until now. And now she's frightened. What if we actually do sell? What would we do then? How would we earn a living? Would there be sufficient income? Is now the time to have a child with all this uncertainty? Now God needs to speak to them, and we need to ask Him for His help. He needs to show them the way.

Anne Marie's from Fort Walton Beach. Placid Gulf. Emerald and sapphire water. White sands. A composition that startles. Shocks in huge sun. Blinds. Hillbilly Riviera, the area's called, but that's to fool beauty lovers. Plain. Flat and plain and sand. Full of plain folks who don't know anything, really. What could they know?

And she is of that place. Graceful in her being as the beach that curves west and east at noon from there. So bright you need to squint, even through sunglasses. Pellucid as the water rising and falling, breathing in and out, against the sand. Gentle as that also, careful as the wading birds that oscillate along the waterline. Joyful as the sound the sand makes against itself as the wind moves it here and there down the long, crystalline, pelican-splashed, salt-smelling day. Generous as the horizon with all that blue.

One could listen to her speak and pray for hour upon hour. The slightly southern, soft, generous voice strolling one through idea after idea, story after story, taking one always back to Jesus, to Yeshua, and to Abba Father, the Great Sea Itself beyond the sea, underlying it, overlaying it, immersing it in Its Being. Her gesture is an opening hand, opening further and further, the wrist opening, unfolding, always.

Early in my coming to the Home Fellowship, she sits with me, after our singing and our Bible study and our praise reports and our prayer requests, after we have broken for dinner, most of the others in the kitchen or dining room or out in the Florida room, saying she understands how it's difficult in a group of new people, difficult to speak. And that's okay. One doesn't need to speak unless one is comfortable with speaking. And she personally is grateful that I have joined the Home Fellowship because there are too few men. It makes it lopsided with all the women they have and so few men. More natural with more men around.

And this is of course a comfort, a great comfort to one alone in a strange state, one's family a thousand miles away. One who is generally quiet, reticent. One who would rather someone else talk than talk himself. Always more interesting that way and easier, less like looking down over the edge of a tall rocky place onto distant small boulders below.

# Barclay

etired minister. Psychotherapist now. Works with clients who have Attention Deficit Disorder, among others. ADD. ADHD.

My fifteen-year-old daughter, Katharine, has ADD. So we have that to talk about.

Open heart patient. One who has been opened up by cutting, snipping, sawing tools. Like Billy.

When he wears shorts, two long scars down his inner thighs and calves where veins have been removed to renovate his heart.

Changed. Disabused. One whose heart has been refurbished from his own, other parts. Reconditioned. Rebuilt.

One imagines the operating theater with the greatest squeamishness. The greatest reluctance.

Fisherman. Intracostal waterway, mostly. Redfish. Sea trout. Others. He brings them to us and cooks them up. Delicious. Just cooked enough. Flaky. Moist. The scent of the ocean from them, the taste of paradise in them, and a sense of a long blue horizon over them. Barclay beaming like a sunup, chewing away, squinting. Old man of the sea. "A bad day fishing is better than a good day doing anything else," he says.

Redfish one night. Cheese grits. Salad. Lovely meal. Another night, sea trout. Salad. Rice. Bread. Delicate. Spiced. Hits the spot.

Daughter speaks in tongues for the first time when she is three. "Evangelical," he declares himself. "Charismatic," he says. Like the rest of us. Fills in for our minister (I'll call him Mark). The minister of our church. Sometimes. Not completely retired, therefore. Hand back into that fire.

He and Jim and Billy on some kitchen committee of Mark's to seek guidance about the national church. Whether we will stay or go. National leadership drifting away from God. Whether we will drift with them or break some way.

Sleep apnea. Just got his machine. My wife, Pat, has the same thing. Nights, she looks like a test pilot. He's getting used to it. Problems. Takes it back. Parts replaced. Adjustments.

Most energy with us Tuesdays and Sundays, he says. Rest of the week he drags. Drags like an anchor through sand.

Acutely conscious of evil. One night, praying over Susan with anointing oil, leading the rest of us, he casts out evil spirits from her that are causing repeated illnesses and troubles at work.

When Twila looks into the faces of singers and worshippers from another church who are visiting our church for conjoined praise and prayer and sees falseness, a fake, a sham, and speaks of this to us at the Home Fellowship, Barclay praises her for her discernment. Her ability to perceive the evil one.

This talk of evil. Spooky to a new Christian. Maybe Barclay senses this. Anyway, that night, after the long discussion of Twila's presentments and visions that have gone on all weekend, as we're breaking for dinner, Barclay says, "Absurd, isn't it, that we're talking about evil and the works of Satan here in the twenty-first century. But here it is. Just as real as he was two thousand years ago."

Hunter. "You will be happy to know I didn't kill Bambi when I was hunting last week." To the Home Fellowship group, recently. "Just hung around in the woods. Good excuse for sitting out there enjoying the outdoors."

Comfortable on the sofa beside Jim. Basketball on the television. "Never been able to work up an interest in basketball. Don't know why."

"I've played basketball all my life. I can't seem to get enough of it," Jim says.

Loose and baggy there with the newspaper on the sofa. Comfortable as a long bulky sweater and old slippers in winter.

Blue eyes. Jowly. Smiles a cocky little boy smile. Cherubic kind of big grin. Hands awkward. Speech halting, then smooth, then halting, then smooth, as though searching for the right set of phrases, sentences, finds them, plays them easily out. Then searches for the next set.

One night speaking of Mark, he's perplexed: "Why hasn't he made better use of me?"

Then, "But God has given me a church. This church," as he looks around at all of us. He laughs, delighted. "You," he said, sweeping his hand through the arc of the room.

In heaven, I imagine Barclay fishing, reclining on a river's grassy bank under a sycamore, maybe, his back against it. And everywhere one looks, in the tree, in the earth, the grass of the earth, the water flowing with the green of the overhanging leaves in it, patches of yellow and white light in it, in Barclay's old clothes and in his red blotchy face, in the quick, soft sounds of the water, in his blue sky eyes, and in the surrounding overgrown fields and woods where the geckos move quietly and doves call and deer tails twitch, there is only God. Barclay and God.

One night teaches that despair, self-castigation, self-condemnation are the work of the evil one. That these, like all Satan's works, need to be cast out immediately. That these are intolerable in ourselves and others. That recognition of one's shortcomings and confession and repentance of one's sins are different, fundamentally. That we are, none of us, perfectible in ourselves but that all of us are perfectible in Jesus. And we need to know this. Know it deeply. That this is an important part of what it means to know Jesus. To be in league with Him. To walk with Him. To hear Him. To speak with Him regularly. To let Him come into our lives fully, completely. To welcome Him. To spend time with Him.

He says these things on a night we meet at Anne Marie's, when Jim and Elaine and Minnie and Billy cannot come. When only Susan, Kim, Twila, Scotty, Kathy, Barclay, and I are present. After I say something like, "As I get older, I am sometimes overwhelmed with how far I fall short." And I am. With how the years have piled up and seem like so many midden layers, how the years that have gone seem sometimes merely an accumulation of my mistakes, my sins, and how the years to come seem likely to be more of the same.

And after Scotty says something like, "I know exactly what you mean, Bill. It's like you are falling down a hole and there's no bottom and the light is disappearing up above. It's like you've lost God and don't know where to look for Him. It's like you can hardly drag yourself through the day sometimes." And the way she says it, everybody looks at one another like, "Look out. The dinghy's sinking. We'd better start bailing!"

And as I sit in Anne Marie's living room, I feel awful for having said something that kicks off what turns out to be an hour and a half of Scotty falling and trying to get a handhold and Barclay offering her his hand and the rest of us offering her our hands.

The point I've tried to make goes unmade, that this conclusion and the despair that accompanies it add another dimension to my need for Jesus. For His help. His forgiveness. His strength to lift the odious weight of myself from my shoulders. The vile, gooey lump of my history. But the point makes no sense when Scotty has moved on to the absence of Jesus, His disappearance from her life.

A bit of a wallow, in other words. And listening to me in my wallow seems to have flipped the wallow switch in her.

But then all of that provokes some marvelous Barclay teaching. Redemptive teaching. A teaching that lifts us up out of ourselves, the graves of our little selfish lives (or my little selfish life, in any event) and into radiance. A brightness that is almost painful. A joyfulness that seems harsh and raucous and rude. That seems at first to bring one up short. To be a kind of rebuke. A sudden discipline.

Open heart surgery. A while back now. Years ago. Thinking of him opened up on an operating table isn't pleasant. Masked, robed technicians milling about, standing about, hovering over the broken, cut open, pried apart, bloody body. An IV dripping. Monitoring equipment. The bright operating room light. The technicians' eyes darting. Their mouths hidden. Clothing crisp as new paper.

Another meeting. Leading the study on Brennan Manning's *The Signature of Jesus*. Trolling for reactions. Thoughts. Asks if we asked Jesus to pray for us, what would we ask Him? Comment: we would probably not ask Him to pray for the thing that He would think we needed Him to pray for. Comment: we would not want to trouble Him with our troubles. Our Savior. Would not want to bother Him. Some laughter at this. Comment: we would want Him to help us find a way to place Him more at the center of our daily lives. Several of us reading passages aloud.

Christianity is dangerous, Manning says. Christians lead dangerous lives. Lives full of pain and joy. Lives loving others. Loving God through others. How do you do that, I ask. How in practical terms does one live that life? Let's be careful here, Barclay says. Let's not be too hard on ourselves.

But I think Manning is quite clear. Here is an exemplary passage from Chapter Six: "There is one spirituality in the Church of the Lord Jesus: paschal spirituality. Essentially it is our daily death to sin, selfishness, dishonesty, and degraded love in order to rise to newness of life. Paul says, 'It is no longer I who live, but Christ lives in me' (Galatians 2:20 NASB). Each time we deal a mortal blow to the ego, the pasch of Jesus is traced in our flesh. Each time we choose to walk the extra mile, to turn the other cheek, to embrace and not reject, to be compassionate and not competitive, to kiss and not bite, to forgive and not massage the latest bruise to our wounded ego, we are breaking through from death to life."

Of course, it's Barclay who suggests this book to us as our next study project. It is he who leads us in the study. Whether he likes it or not, he has exposed us to a light of the brightest intensity. A light that burns away the inessential and illuminates the essential. No matter that he also tries to keep us safe from its burning.

For a few weeks in the summer, he is Mark's fill-in. The stand-in pastor for Mark, who is on vacation. A comfort up there, the old pastor. Faithful as a pastor may be. Thirty-five years ago, he took his vows. Bad knees. Bad heart. But he keeps on with the service. Can't sleep. Hard to walk. Hard to stand. Yet week after week, he offers up prayers.

One Sunday service, he notes the absence of many. Sick. Under spiritual attack. He asks us all to recognize what is going on. That many are being attacked by Satan's forces. While he may have already lost, he may still inflict damage. We must claim our authority in the name of Jesus, he says. We must claim the power of Jesus and His blood as our own in this war. Let us pray with His authority that our afflictions are lifted. Let us make it a point to pray the collect for today during the coming week.

Redfish and trout. Flat water fish in the space between barrier islands and the Florida mainland that like it where springs well up and rivers flow into the salt. Shallows fish that may go eight or ten pounds and that are a pure feistiness in the catching. And the way he prepares them on the grill or in the oven—just done but no more—with olive oil and salt and pepper and some others, they seem a heavenly gift. Straight from Barclay and Jesus to us. No worldly tincture. Nothing from the world in them to spoil their flavor. Just a delicate, substantial sweetness one might reasonably expect.

He carries himself as though he had a tender and somewhat delicate cargo, as though to turn his neck too quickly might snap it, as though too vigorous a step might break a leg or a hip or a rib. And in his face the way he carries his heavy body is as though he would rather it not be the difficulty it now proves to be, the obstruction it now has turned into, but would rather it become something more like what he may remember in the moments when the aches and the weariness go dull enough for memory to be stronger. Or perhaps it is imagination rather than memory, and he imagines in brief times between clock ticks that he becomes as weightless and well as he imagines dead saints to be. Or maybe it is neither. Maybe as he makes his way carefully through the world now, through this painful world as slow as a man walking on the bottom of the sea, he is lifted from time to time by Jesus at his elbow and finds infinite relief.

Another Home Fellowship. Barclay's in long pants, and there's a stain on his pants below his knee on his left leg. Asked how he is: "Not all that well. I fell over the weekend getting from one place to another in the boat. Kind of embarrassing, but there it is."

"Looks like it hurts."

"Yes it does."

"But did you catch anything?" I asked.

"No, I didn't. It wasn't much of a day."

Later, he's absent with Elaine, as she cleans and soaks and bandages. Then earlier than normal, he shuffles out, his jaw working almost imperceptibly under his departing smile.

Another Home Fellowship. As we discuss my upcoming home purchase, Barclay offers me a few books he has on native flora. "What you want is plants that don't need a lot of water. Remind me when you move in, and I'll loan them to you."

Another Home Fellowship. "I used to live out in the country until about a year ago. Beautiful. Away from all these cars and the city. But it got to be. . . . physically, I just couldn't do it." As he says this, he looks away. There is a look to his eyes as though he were regarding something at a distance. Something not at all in the room. He lives in an apartment now.

Another Home Fellowship. Several times over a period of many months, he asks for prayer for me and my family as we endure the time apart. He asks for prayer that all will go well with us. That our home selling and home buying will go quickly and smoothly.

Everyone puts these prayers on their prayer cards. And it does. It all does go well. And I praise God at praise time that all has indeed gone well. Thank everyone. Thank God for answered prayer. I have a friend who moves from the same town and cannot sell his house for more than a year, who carries two mortgages. Something I could not do.

Our old house sells to the first person who looks at it. And our new house closes without any significant surprises, a house all of us like. The garage is too small, and storage is non-existent. But we knew that going in. No house is perfect. One accepts the virtues along with the deficiencies.

But as with people, houses sometimes hide their short-comings. Shortly after we move in, one Sunday morning, the toilets refuse to flush and Katharine's shower drain backs up. Pat works on the toilets with a plunger. We miss church. I call the former owners—Tom and Sally, I'll call them—and wake them. They don't know anything except a thickness in their tongues. I call several septic tank companies. Leave messages on answering machines. As the day proceeds, the toilets begin to flush tentatively. One contractor agrees to evaluate the situation Monday, relieved he doesn't have to work on Sunday.

Monday we learn from Sally who put in the field two years before. Someone comes out from that company too. A week later, after much phoning around, negotiating, digging in our yard—"exploratory surgery" one trouble-shooter calls it—and after looking down into a tank of one's excrement on a few occasions, after cutting and leveling and inclining and declining everyone declares himself done, and we're back to normal except for the dug-up looking yard. And the lingering, heightened awareness of the excrement one makes and where it goes and how it gets there and how it might all be doing down there, how delicate plumbing systems really are, and how it is all just outside, in one's front yard. And how when one thinks one is rid of something, has cast it out, one may have it with one in some measure for a very long time, just there, over the hedge and under the grass.

And so while one thanks God for answered prayer, one also thanks God for reminders of what one is without Him and how delicate one's earthly household is and how one is blessed, blessed beyond reason, with physics one can actually depend on for the most part when a job is done right. Physics that He supplies, an orderliness that He loves and keeps for us.

Another Home Fellowship. Most of the summer, Barclay's subdued. Not saying much of anything. Coming, quietly praying, eating his dinner, and then going home.

For awhile he's gone from church, but then comes back. It's good when he comes back.

Barclay's Birthday Party. Sixty-five. Sixty-five big ones, the invitation says. And it seems he's lost some weight. Looks good, presider in his daughter's house. Honorable and the honored. Someone asks early on if his daughter is married or his son, who are both busy about the place with food and drink. And he says, "No. Both of my children have had the good sense not to marry." And then he laughs.

Gradually I hear that he will be leaving soon on a hunting trip to Colorado. Elk. Two weeks away. And his blue eyes shine about like lakes full of glacial run-off as he talks about it and his preparations for it.

Anne Marie's there and tells about a kitten she's just brought home: "An infant substitute," she says, laughing.

45

And the way she describes it curling up against her chest and neck, she makes clear that's exactly what it is. She's lost ten pounds, she says, because of the anti-depressants. She looks okay but maybe a little tired, changed in a manner that isn't clear. Less light in the eyes. The negotiations with the buyers of the restaurant continue.

"Seems like this has been going on a long time," I say.

"Yes," she quickly replies. Almost a year." She describes contract clauses and certified letters, negotiating strategy, and monthly sales.

"Problem is," she says, "we're down five percent for September but fourteen percent for October. I think they'll want to renegotiate the price because of Nine-Eleven. I've told Michael he'll need to come up with a bottom line number. Otherwise we won't know whether we should sell or not, when they come back with their new number."

When I ask, she says Michael wanted to stay home to watch the game. World series game. I don't have the sports gene; so I don't even think I know who's playing, much less who is up how many, and the game is on there right in front of me, with Jim and Robert and Barclay and some of the others facing directly toward it. Toward the mostly blue-lighted and green-lighted glass.

Tori's there. Light. Buoyant. Her brown-blond hair long down her shoulders in ringlets. Talks about her statuary work. Mainly her Statue of Liberty work. How hard that is, holding the torch up there all night, no matter how light they make it. How these days there are a lot of people throwing parties with a patriotic theme. And then there is her mermaid work. Which she sometimes does lying down, flipping her tail occasionally. Or sitting.

Elaine's lively. Says maybe when the Alpha course is over at the church, it would be better for her to do the Home Fellowship on Wednesday nights because of her (literally) heavy workload on Mondays and Tuesdays, both heavy and long. Especially since the women like to stay late. She calls them girls. The single women I think she means. And maybe those who want to do Tuesdays can continue going to Minnie and Billy's, and those who like Wednesdays can come to her place. Well, we are quite large now, and maybe some kind of splitting away would make sense. Perhaps would be practical. But it's not a happy thought.

Then Barclay's son comes into the group of us eating our barbeque—Elaine, Tori, Pat, Scotty, and me—and asks if he can get us anything. "You know," Elaine says. "You are such a gracious host for asking. You put on such a lovely party. We're all having a wonderful time."

"I'm glad," he says, big smile and dimples.

"You know, you're good-looking enough to be President," Elaine says, laughing.

We all laugh and then pause to hear what she might say next. But before she can, Ben speaks: "Thank you. I think." Then he wanders off to get someone something somewhere.

"I don't believe I said that," Elaine says. "I never know what's going to come out of my mouth next."

"It must be more exciting that way," I respond, laughing again with the rest.

"It certainly is. To say the least."

In the kitchen, later, Susan discusses work. Current and past. Goes all the way back to college, answering my questions, my journalistic pokes, through which I learn that she majored in German. Surprised because I just figured she had majored in English. But no. She'd stayed clear of that to avoid her father (and his English department) who gives one the impression that after Shakespeare and Milton and others it's pretty hard these days for writers to measure up. Whatsoever. And I learn that she worked as a technical writer for a local defense contractor for a couple of years and that she was a free-lancer for a few years as well. All animated. Wine glass waving about, mostly empty. The words all flowing easy as spring water down a fall.

And I learn that she's sent out writing of her own for the first time. Ever. Poems. Children's poems. Consequent to Ed's two evenings of poetry readings and discussion at the Home Fellowship. Consequent to her combination family reunion and summer vacation, during which she spent much happy time with her sister's children. But she asks that I keep this secret because she doesn't want the others taking up the topic. Then later I stupidly ask her something about it within Elaine's overhearing, and now her cheeks flush, and I am chastened. Elaine isn't sure what she's heard. So now Susan whispers the whole thing or some part of it into Elaine's ear and extracts her promise as well.

Barclay's children move from room to room. Lubricating the conversation at first and then moving the food and drink and various implements around as the conversation becomes self-lubricating. Their mother must be tall and quite beautiful, we say to one another. Or if we do not say it to one another, we say it to ourselves. She lives in town, but we do not know her. And by knowing Barclay, we don't know what to think we do or don't know of her. We only know that if she is half as gracious and apparently kind and outgoing and smart and engaging and courteous as Barclay's children, Barclay and God are both greater mysteries than we'd thought.

# Billy

On my first morning at the church, as I approach the informal welcome area that begins the breezeway back toward the church itself, Billy comes at me, big as one of those new Volkswagens under the ballistic, parabolic blue dome of Florida sky. He shakes my hand and continues shaking until he's loosened my story from me like so much change. I cannot remember now exactly what he says or how he holds his hands or mouth, but it does strike me how much Billy wishes me to like his little church, set there in a modest stand of skinny pines by the side of a busy road. Swelling as though it belongs to him personally. The way someone would like it very much if you would like a home he had especially built to accommodate guests, guests like you.

Frog of a prince. Prince of a frog. Croak-croak. Ribbit. Croak. He works at it. Not easy croaking. Convincingly. Day in. Day out.

Billy. Billy Goat Gruff. One minister calls him.

God makes us all ways. I think of Paul. A pistol. A genuine pain. Professionally obnoxious. Expertly irritating. I do not boast, he says. I have my authority from God. Can you imagine? Yet it was precisely this outrageousness that was called for. Called for certainly by God. To take the church forward. Out of Israel and into the world.

Deep knowledge of Scripture. Perhaps as deep as Minnie's, although it's hard to tell.

Prays like this. "Holy Father, please protect Mary-Maud while she is in jail and keep her children just as safe as You kept David when he slew Goliath. Please heal Bill's mother miraculously of her emphysema, and give Bill Your confidence and comfort there in his apartment, away from his family. We also pray for Travis, Twila's husband, that over time he will come to know and acknowledge You, Lord, and will come to discover great joy in that knowledge. Finally, we pray for the little babies of Barclay's friend, that they are born healthy and that their mother, following delivery, remains healthy. We ask these things in Jesus' precious name. Amen."

One night, the subject of sexual relations comes up in the Home Fellowship. Perhaps Billy's brought it up. Perhaps a Biblical reference. Billy says, "Well, that's not happening. I'll tell you that. No way. Not anymore for us, you know. Ha, ha, ha! Not in the cards. No, sir!"

A few of us laugh. "You laugh, but I'm telling you the truth!"

Minnie looks down at her hands in her lap. Her head wobbles slightly on the thin end of her neck. Eyes almost closed. Smiles.

Another night. Speaks about younger days, his children still ungrown, running all over the house half-dressed. Yelling down the stairs, "Bus leaves for church in ten minutes. You'd better hurry. Ten minutes."

The silliness of it. How foolish he was. "Then I realized I didn't need to do that. I could help her get them ready." And then, "What a change there was after that. What a difference."

Minnie looks down into her hands in her lap. Her head wobbles. Eyes almost closed. Smiles.

Another night. Says, "Minnie sometimes can't even find her way back home."

"That's not true," she says, the *oooo* sound strung out for emphasis.

"Of course it's true," says Billy. "You know what I'm talking about, don't you?"

"Well. Let me tell him the whole story, won't you?"

"Ha, ha, ha! Why do you want to do that? It'll just show him I'm right. It'll just show him you really can't find your way home."

"Bill, it was like this. I was following June back to her house because she was going to drop something off, but I didn't know where she lived. So I was following her, but I didn't notice that a car like hers slipped between us after we turned, you know, and I started thinking that car was her car, when it wasn't. June turned. I don't know when. I didn't see it. But the other car kept going.

"It went all over the place. Places in town I've never been before. Bill, I didn't recognize were I was. I guess I got kind of scared.

"Pretty soon, the car turns into a driveway and stops. Somebody gets out. A stranger. It isn't June. So I back out. But I don't know which way to go."

"So she calls me on her cell phone."

"I'm telling it, Billy."

"She calls me on her cell phone and asks directions! Ha, ha, ha! Hee-hee-hee!"

"Well, I didn't know where I was. I'd gotten turned around, you see. I was on a road I knew, but I didn't know where I was on it. Which direction I was going. What part of town I was in."

"I'll tell you which way she was going. She was going the wrong way."

"Yes," she says, smiling knowingly. "I was going the wrong way. But Billy helped me. I called him, and after that I was able to find my way home again." Saying "again" with a long a on both syllables, like the English. "Thank you, Billy."

"After I gave you directions."

"Yes. That's right"

Another night. Says, "In Virginia, we grew enormously. The evangelism. I took training in it. We had John Wimber come in. Then we trained others. There are techniques, you know. You can learn the signs that someone wants to be saved. That's when you apply those techniques, you see. When there's that inclination there, that slight leaning. That's when you go in and pluck a soul for the Lord.

"Ho, ha! Those were the days. We grew and grew. I was business manager. Some weeks we counted twenty-five thousand from the plate.

"We tried it here, but it didn't work the same. I don't know. I think it has to do with the clergy. I think they like things as they are here, most of them. There isn't the support.

"No. We didn't make anybody do anything. You can tell when people want to accept the Lord. We only worked on those. The rest we said good-bye to. Said here's where we are. Stop by. This is what we're about. We'd love to see you. Wrote them off. If they showed up, fine. Otherwise, okay too. Up to them."

But it's always, "William. How are you?" A willingness to listen. A fatherly interest in whatever may be happening, whatever the latest perturbation would be. A continuous sense that we are Christians together in this, whatever will surface.

One day, church. Pale. Shaky. Heart. Clogged arteries. Had open heart, like Barclay, already. "Had my last one," he said. "Last operation on this thing," he said, knocking on his chest. "The one and only. I'm not going through that again."

Vague about the doctors. He goes. We all know he goes. But the upshot isn't clear. What's to be done? What can be done? What will be done? What should be done? Having no other particular leverage, we pray that whatever can be done, will be done. That whatever is pleasing to God will also take Billy's ailment away. Subsequently, he colors for a time, and all of us are sanguine.

One evening at the Home Fellowship, Billy's about to leave. (If he doesn't leave now and stays later, he won't be able to sleep.) "Before I was saved," he says, "I was worldly. Ha, ho, ha, ho! Oh yes. I was a worldly son of a gun. Ask anybody. An-y-bo-dy. They'll tell you," he says. Leaves.

The only person I can think to ask is Minnie, and I'm not sure I want to do that. She's still there. They've driven separately. She'll be around for awhile.

At our church's annual meeting, Billy sits with me in the back, the next-to-last row. "In the back, with the sinners," he says. Carol reviews the budget projected up on the screen we use when we're singing praise songs.

"I made a big fuss last year," he says. "I was chair of the outreach committee. I quit in protest. Stood right up as Carol was reviewing the budget, just as she's doing now. And just quit in front of God and everybody. Disgusted." He says this last with his lips shaped in a shape of disgust. A few people turn their heads to look at us because of Billy's talking. But Billy politely pays no attention to them.

"Look at how much of the budget is in outreach," he says. He points to the columns of figures projected up on the screen over the altar. "Peanuts. Five percent. Absurd. It should be fifty percent. I told them that last year. Then I quit. I'm out of it now. They can do whatever they want to do, just as long as they give fifty percent of what I give to outreach. And if they won't honor that request, I'll quit."

"Quit?"

"Yes. Quit. Again. Hee, hee, hee. Only quit the whole thing. I'll find another church."

He raises his voice for everyone to hear clearly, everyone in Florida and west Texas too. "I'm ashamed to belong to a church that gives so little to the poor."

"But Billy," Mark says. "Billy, no one is preventing you from contributing whatever you believe you should. It's a matter of mission. The church has certain missions that it has taken on."

"What does Jesus say about the poor? Oughtn't we to be following Jesus?"

"Jesus has led us to the missions we are involved with, Billy. That is how we have arrived where we are today, by praying for and receiving guidance."

"I'm disgusted, but I'm going to be quiet now. You go on with your meeting. I'll be quiet now."

Another Home Fellowship. Back from the doctor and back from the doctor again. A glow now in his cheeks. "Still can't lift hardly anything," he says, but he allows as how he is feeling better. Looks like he might survive awhile after all. We praise God for answered prayer.

Another Home Fellowship. Misses the week before attending his sister's funeral in Texas, where he's from. Say I am sorry to hear she has died. "She was sick a long time," he said. "Alzheimer's. Went on for years."

"She's better now," he says. "Thank God."

"Thank you," I said. He looks surprised.

"For what?"

"For dinner last week."

"Oh. I heard the mussels were good."

"They were. Thank you. And so was the jazz."

"I'm glad. Sorry I missed it."

Home Fellowship Christmas party. Curly brown wig. Name tag saying "Brett" covering a shirt button.

Looking about the room at the familiar people, the strangers. Food on his plate. Munching. Thoughtfully. Thinking of something funny to say, maybe. Anne Marie engages him. Elaine. Later Susan. Twila. Still later, Kathy. Scotty. Kim. He enjoys them, clearly. All these younger women. Pretty too. Smiling. Laughing. Haw, haw, haw! Babe magnet, if ever there was one.

Some time later, the wig is put away. Sits momentarily by himself in the temporarily empty living room. Looking out a window into the street. Reflected in it, people in the distant dining room. Florida room. Car goes by. What he's thinking, one may only speculate. Arrangements and rearrangements, perhaps. Comings and goings. Birthings and dyings. Seasons passing. Conversions. Lights going on and off. Suns rising and setting, moons rising and setting. Clouds passing. Or nothing. Another car goes by. Loud nothing, rushing like a wind come in from the Atlantic. Or the memory of one. A Texas wind, maybe. Dry and dusty. Rolling across asphalt and hardpan, lifting what's loose. Spinning it. Twisting it out. Thrusting it up. Away.

Another Home Fellowship. He asks for prayer for Minnie. For her epigastric reflux. For this difficulty she's had for years but never known what to call, never known what to do about except to keep quiet. And he offers praise that the doctor has finally discovered this and can help her, can improve her, can medicate that particular ailment.

Another Home Fellowship. He asks for prayer for Minnie whose foot is a problem, whose foot no longer fits in her shoe, for which she is getting a specially made shoe to reduce the pain. He asks for healing and for a shoe that is effective in reducing the pain. He says effective emphatically, long e on the start of the word, the *fec* part almost an expletive.

# Carol

New to the Home Fellowship. Almost a year now after I arrive. Old in the church. Years old, countable on one or two hands. Red hair. Humble. Smiles. Always busy. On some errand or mission. For someone. Questions a Vestry member in the breezeway. Then returns to the computer in the Church office. Keyboards there. Quickly. Intently.

Works in the church part time. Finance and accounting. Full time somewhere else. Lives alone with her young son. Jake. Nine. Ten. Eleven.

Third night, maybe, she testifies. Her story typed on papers in her hands and under them her Bible.

Present: Elaine and Jim, Barclay, Robert and Lucy, Susan, Kim, Scotty. Me. Later on, Twila. Absent: Billy and

63

Minnie (entertaining grandchildren on vacation), Anne Marie (who is, I hope, somewhere else good), Kathy (who is training in Colorado), and others I do not think of.

A short story that covers a lot of territory, from coal-mining grandfather in Pennsylvania to school to the party phase out in California with her husband, staying up four and five days at a time, playing cards. Having a good time.

Nervous, as she tells this. The papers rustling. Rustling. On the spot. This goes on for years and years.

As it does, an evil presence. Sometimes it seems to be coming from the cards, the playing cards, the edges of the room, other people. Demons, maybe. A battle. Ongoing battle. She wins but just.

Gradually, she finds she doesn't want to live like this. It goes from fun to not so fun to no fun to terrible.

Gradually, she wants out. Speaks to her husband, but he's still in the fun phase. Still loving the rush of it, the wildness, the glamour of this life. The fame of it. All the jazz greats party with them, their circle, when they're in town. One enormous jazz party. One long intellectual, playful, sensual, light-hearted, heavy-headed dalliance and drift.

Then one night, unsleeping, staring up at the ceiling, husband asleep, wondering whether this feeling will ever end and how she might bring it to an end, knowing she cannot, on her own, ever bring this to an end, this attack on her, she notices Him out of the corner of an eye standing there with his arms open to her. She turns and looks. Raises up on an elbow. In the corner. Quiet as a stone or a sky with no wind or a whale diving one mile down.

Not a ghostly presence. Not a vagueness lifted from her imagination. No swamp gas. No vapors. Nothing foggy or spooky or odd or ephemeral. Just Him. Only Him. Jesus looking straight into her. The real Jesus. All there. Jesus in his body and his body there, in her bedroom, standing in the corner. His actual body. His actual person.

They stare at one another. Then He rises. Finger in the air for some reason surely, but who knows what it is. Disappears through the ceiling.

Then shortly after this she discovers she is pregnant. She carries the baby, wondering. Then the doctor tells her he cannot detect a heartbeat. Says she should have a D&C. The fetus is dead.

She does not believe this. God gives her boldness in this matter. She quickly gets a second opinion. This one finds the heartbeat. There will be no D&C.

The fetus turns out to be Jake, who I watch search for Easter eggs at the church on Easter Sunday a few months before. Good kid. A little skinny. A lot of kneecaps and elbows, like photos show me to have been when I was his age. Who takes karate and is working diligently toward his black belt. Whose close-cut hair looks a little like the Princeton haircuts I used to get at his age. My father would order for me.

As she finishes, Carol is crying. We're silenced. All of us. Like a desert running out to the horizon.

Elaine asks us all to pray over Carol. She kneels by Carol's chair. Several of us congregate around her, a couple of us touching her, a couple of us with a palm held out toward her, one or two just standing, arms at our sides, a few others still sitting on chairs with heads bowed. We pray, asking God's blessing on her and Jake, thanking Him for her saving, her testimony, asking Him to care for her.

Sorrow is a hard thing in a Christian, a rough, ir-regular, shrapnel-sharp thing. A loud, oily, screeching, machine-like thing. A hard thing to see in another, to hear. To smell and to taste and to touch. Even harder in oneself. Because they just don't go together. Don't be-long together. Like Jesus and Hitler.

Sorrow in anyone is hard, because we aren't made for that. We're made for joy and love.

Sorrow is love's ruin, joy's banishment.

But Christians are supposed to be drinking the Ultimate Joy Juice and should therefore be overwhelmed by love. Twenty-four seven. Vibrating with joy. Immersed in the warm, cosmic ocean of God.

But for most of us, Carol and me included, it isn't that way. There is sorrow and pain, still, interspersed with the sense of God's intimate presence, His hands around us, sheltering us, His breath upon us like a breeze through orange groves and jasmine beds.

This intermittent experience of God's presence, this periodicity, is of course our doing and is a sign of our brokenness. Or inattention. Which is the same thing. And the sorrow we encounter is a reminder to us of what it is like to be separate from God and is an impetus to our seeking a closer relationship with Him.

As others have said, there is a blessing in sorrow. For it encourages a return to God. And this return is, of course, prayer. Something I'm only beginning to learn something about. The practice of the presence of God, as Brother Lawrence calls it. The sacrament of the present moment, as Jean-Pierre de Caussade calls it.

In its extreme form, in its perfect form, it is prayer that is constant, continual. Uninterrupted. Unmodified in its intimacy by one's other conversations and activities. One's other activities and conversations become part of one's conversation with God, become expressions to God of one's

love for Him and one's thankfulness for His many blessings.

One reads books. As a new Christian, one devours books
about Grace, about discipleship, about the Gospel. One
reads one's Bible. One attends Bible classes or study groups.
One attends one's Home Fellowship. One prays.

And after a time, after some months or maybe a year
of this, one begins to discern a marked difference between the periods when one is praying often and for significant periods of time and when one is not so much.
There may be many reasons for the variability. Work
pressure. Family needs. Illness. Vacation. There may be
reasons one gives oneself for drifting away from God,
not spending time with Him.

But the inevitable result for me is that I am less joyful, less loving, less understanding, less patient, and less
happy. More prone toward moodiness, irritability, anger, depression, and sadness. More sensitive to the
bumps and bruises of everyday life.

Jesus and Hitler. How what apparently doesn't go together does, when God's love enters in. Cascades in.

Sorrow and pain flood out when we experience ourselves in our separateness, when the random scrap metal
of a chaotic universe rains on our heads. On the flood of

our tears, our helplessness, our sorrow and pain are carried out of us and into the sensibilities of those around us.

Sorrow and pain are not altogether autonomic. There's some choice involved. Very little, sometimes. Much, others. An exercise of will. Will that can turn us either toward or away from God, can take us into the ocean of His being or out of that ocean far inland. And the farther inland we take ourselves, the greater our pain. The greater our sense of defeat and isolation.

We do have a choice when events lop off a limb or crush a bone. We can take our body to the Great Physician, or we can retreat into the cave of ourselves and nurse the pain, perhaps even fan the fire of it.

Carol has brought her pain to the Great Physician, to God in us, as we all do here in this Home Fellowship. Bent over often as we approach Elaine's house, we drag our pain like so many heavy sacks behind us.

After her testimony, over a plate of food in front of us, on our knees, we small talk. Carol. Susan. I ask about schools and degrees and stuff like that. It's good having Susan there. Balancing my curiosity with her opinions and funny stories. Carol's tears have gone. Laughs quietly. Happily. Turns out she has a technical degree and an MBA. I'm surprised. I don't know why. Soon. Sooner than most. She's gone.

Church. Couple of weeks later. We stop and talk in the breezeway. Early July. Warm.

Jake's still out west. He'll be gone a month altogether, visiting with his father. And she's resting from all the soccer. Relaxing. Taking a bit of time Saturdays to lunch with a friend. The last two. A vacation for her too. Sort of. Two weeks, and she's ready for him, to come back. Sees no reason why he can't come back home now. Gets a feeling of what it will be like when he leaves for college and then for good. How her life is wholly about his now. Or almost. And how that will need to change someday. But it can't, of course. Because one's child always is one's child.

Comes to half a dozen evenings or so. Then must stop. Jake's back. School starts, and Tuesdays something else is going on.

We're talking in the breezeway. It's early September. Warm still. Elaine says she needs fellowship, and this is very clear. She totally agrees with this. But Tuesdays won't work with her schedule. Wednesday would work. Maybe she could come to Alpha, the Alpha course we will be giving in a couple of weeks. (A course in what Christianity is about for non-Christians and for new Christians. A refresher course for some. A reminder. Also a back to basics for those who got confused along the way. Dinner, a video, then small groups.) That's what Elaine says, she says. Well? Maybe, she says. We'll see.

Alpha. First night, she is there. Upbeat. Busy as ever. When she moves by, as I listen to a newcomer talk about his career in the Army, his retirement, his children, his current job as a bus driver, I wonder how this will turn out, this person, this story unfolding among us, this soul, this mother and son—their two souls—this tentative, extravagant tenderness. This devotion. This Love.

# Darren

Not his real name. In and out. Jim's work friend. Forties. Friendly. Cheerful. Quiet as a power-saving computer in power-save mode. Chit chats well. Wife moves out. After talk of it a month before. Then a what-am-I-doing phase, of-course-I-love-you. Ernest talks late into the night. Tired-looking the few times he comes. Calm as an alarm clock. May I pray with you, he wants to know. And of course we welcome him to pray with us and share small talk and big talk too. Sometimes he's here, and sometimes he's not. We pray for him. Then he doesn't come, and there isn't any news. Then he has moved to Texas. Started a new life there.

# Ed

Starts out like me. Quiet as the center of a stone. Begins about the time Carol begins, along with Lucy and Robert. Big guy. Commutes to work Mondays through Fridays to where we are from somewhere else. Rents a small apartment.

Wife at home. Son just gone off to college, and he doesn't want them to move so that he can come home and visit with his friends. Daughter off at college too for a couple of years now. Likes literature, like he did. Headed that way. Has a head for science, though, which he'd like her to do something about. More secure a living, he thinks.

An attorney. Works for someone else. Had his own firm but gave it up. Too much fussing and administrative stuff.

Christian all his life, one would think, by the depth and breadth of his knowledge of Christian things. History. Scripture. Christian writings. Liturgical music. All of these. Regularly tosses off questions or comments or answers or replies that are revelations to me, the new boy in this, the awkward acolyte.

Friendly. Talkative, but interesting. Informative without any apparent intention to condescend. Wanting merely to share a fascinating bit of something. Like a man who reaches into his case to produce a gold-flecked gem or the skin of some exotic animal or a very small car with doors that really open and close and a steering wheel that actually turns the front wheels. Here, take a look at this. Try it. Take it, and try it out. See what you think. Amazing, isn't it? Truly amazing how every detail is correct. Proportionate. Exquisite. As if a small world existed outside of ourselves made up of small people who make these things for themselves, for their actual use.

Voice like an announcer's. Not practiced, really, so much as born that way. Some people are born to announce things, and Ed is one. Not loud but unambiguous, clear in what it purports. A straight line from beginning to end. A heavy black line from subject to predicate and on through the short subordinated clauses. No fuss. No tangents. From A to B along the most direct path.

Literature major. But he left that behind until a few years ago when he picked up a book by John Ciardi: *How Does a Poem Mean?* Read it through three times or so. Then he went back to literature, especially poems. Most particularly Christian poets and poets who take on Christian themes. Made a new study in his middle age. And brought out a pamphlet of about ten poems from Gerard Manley Hopkins, George Herbert, W.B. Yeats, and others, which he used for teaching high school students in his church.

Elaine asks him to lead the Home Fellowship in a study, and he chooses to use the pamphlet that he used with the high school students at church years ago. We take two nights to get through it. Refreshing to revisit all that, to talk literature for the first time, really, in decades with anyone, outside of family—Ken and his kids. Not that I do much talking. It's Ed mostly, and some of the others.

If I were asked to vote, I'd say just stay with Hopkins. Can't get enough of him. Ed goes through "God's Grandeur" and "Spring and Fall." A few days later, I am re-reading "The Windhover," "Pied Beauty," "Harry Ploughman," "(Carrion Comfort)," "Binsey Poplars," and "Wreck of the Deutschland." Hopkins, whom I don't know I've especially missed until I'm presented with him again.

"Pied Beauty" is probably my favorite:

Glory be to God for dappled things—
For skies of couple-colour as a brindled cow;
For rose-moles all in stipple upon trout that swim;
Fresh-firecoal chestnut-falls; finches' wings;
Landscape plotted and pieced—fold, fallow, and plough;
And all trades, their gear and tackle and trim.

All things counter, original, spare, strange:
Whatever is fickle, freckled (who knows how?)
With swift, slow; sweet, sour; adazzle, dim;
He fathers-forth whose beauty is past change:
Praise him.

Oh, ho. What loveliness! What prodigious mining!
What are Herbert and Yeats beside this man who digs
bare-handed through hundreds of yards of rock and
dirt—knuckle-busting, nail-tearing work—until he has
several heavy gold nuggets to offer one at a time, until
you have them all yourself in the palm of your hand, and
then he turns to go back digging again to find you more.

Well, but of course I have great regard for Herbert and
Yeats also. In the batch of poems Ed goes through is Yeats'
"The Mother of God:"

The threefold terror of love; a fallen flare
Through the hollow of an ear;
Wings beating about the room;
The terror of all terrors that I bore
The Heavens in my womb.

Had I not found content among the shows
Every common woman knows,
Chimney corner, garden walk,
Or rocky cistern where we tread the clothes
And gather all the talk?

What is this flesh I purchased with my pains,
This fallen star my milk sustains,
This love that makes my heart's blood stop
Or strikes a sudden chill into my bones
And bids my hair stand up?

After someone reads the poem—maybe Anne Marie—Billy rereads the first stanza and says, "Even though he might not have been a Christian, God was surely helping old Mister—who is it—Yeats in through there. You can hear Him, can't you? 'The Heavens in my womb.' I can, and that's a fact." And as he says this, you get the feeling his heart has certainly been touched.

A septuagenarian Texan with a degree in business and a career in the Pentagon in budgetary planning. Then work as a church finance and accounting guy. Also now, as it turns out, a student of poetry.

Of course, it's the mystery. The great silent roaring spinning stillness that is God is not really comprehensible in the way one normally goes at things. With math, for example. Or logic: All men are mortal; Socrates was a man; Socrates was mortal. Or evidence of either the historical or scientific variety. Or sensation, as in knowledge through direct (I'm being a little disingenuous here) experience with one's five senses.

It's God's mystery that poetry gets at best. Mystery's the beginning of belief and the center of it. And when one wants to understand that mystery better, one goes to poetry or literature that rises to the poetic. The Bible is one, certainly. But if God is Love itself, among other things, one is hard-pressed to find any well-wrought literature that is not about Him in some way, either His presence or His absence or His opposite or an echo of Him. Directly or indirectly. Most often and most effectively, indirectly.

One sometimes gets the sense of an infinite ravel, as though everything were arranged in one long continuous strand—all pain, all joy, all love, all hate, all indifference, all life, all death—and that as one touches one part of the strand the remainder of it vibrates. The full length. But that at its center, twisted all the way through it, like some other-worldly super-conductor of the Creator's very Being, stronger than titanium and more flexible than flax, is Love.

Another Home Fellowship—game night—Ed and Jim and I retreat into the Florida room, which used to be a screened-in porch but is now enclosed, the women remaining in the living room in two groups, each playing a different game. Cards in one and pictures of some sort in the other. Jim presses us to play Trivial Pursuit. I say I'm not really a game player. I'd be happy to watch, I say, but he continues to press and I give in. After all, there's only two of them, and three would be better, and I'm tired of playing the odd man out.

But I'm lousy at games, all games. Golf, for example. Scrabble. Bowling. Bridge. Miserably bad. Give me a game that depends only on luck and no knowledge, then I'll do okay. I would not say do well. I enter into this game knowing I'll lose.

The evening proceeds. Ed collects the little pie shaped slices in his round pie-shaped plastic game-piece-thing. Luck (or what we think of as luck) is against him, while knowledge is with him. His bad luck keeps him from landing on the spaces he needs to land on to get all his little pie shaped pieces, but along the way he answers just about everything correctly.

Jim and I struggle. Luck is with us. We land on the correct spaces to get the pie pieces, but we don't know the answers. We get a few right, but Ed gets five right to our one. Finally, I must leave. Jim and I forfeit to Ed, who has twice the number of little pie shaped pieces that we do. We are both happy to finally end it, the long confrontation with our ignorance. Still, it is good to share even this, this evening of ambivalence.

Another Home Fellowship. Ed tells the story of a friend who he hasn't spoken to in years but reads about in the paper. Another attorney whom he came to know and like, when they were adversaries in a trial. Ed was the researcher on his side. His friend was lead on his. Went on to be very prominent, earning an excellent income. Wife divorced him, leaving him with the kids. A few years later, he remarried, the woman having children from a previous marriage. Continued to do well. Then a decade or decade and a half later, now, Ed reads about how he has done absolutely nothing on a *pro bono* case, has been taken off the case, and is being considered for disciplinary action by the Florida Bar. Is being publicly humiliated. Calls the guy up to see how he's doing.

Discovers the guy's life is in a shambles. His second wife has left him, having testified in the divorce proceedings against him that she only married him because of the income he could provide. Now he has virtually no income, because of his having steadily disintegrated since his second wife left him and since the Florida Bar's consideration of disciplinary action has made it difficult to find work. Lives in a small apartment alone. Has visitation rights with the child he had with his second wife, a twelve-year-old. Ed invites them to a youth group outing sponsored by his church. They go, have a good time. At the end of the day, the guy is embarrassingly grateful. Clearly this is the best thing that has happened to him in quite awhile.

"He's well-educated. Smart. Has been very successful. And here he is. Nearly destitute. Abandoned by two wives. The best thing that has happened to him in a long time is that he gets invited to a picnic. One wonders how this can be, sometimes. How such suffering can make sense."

"Is he a Christian?" Barclay wants to know.

"Yes he is."

We quietly consider this. "How is his relationship with the Lord?"

"I honestly don't know."

Later, during prayers, we pray for Ed's friend. "Sometimes we don't know why these things happen, Lord," Ed says. "But they do, and we trust that You will work things out."

Suffering is frightening. I wonder about the safety of my children and wife, the well-being of my parents and brothers and sister. I pray for them all.

My sister has just gone through the death of her ex-husband, Jim. They divorced a few years ago, after she moved to London. Why isn't clear. Late last summer, cancer. For a time, through last fall and most of the winter, he had trouble accepting the fact that he was dying. But she and his doctor finally got through to him.

She took a few long vacations over a period of eight or ten months to be with him and help him. He had no contact with his family. Something terrible happened many years ago, and there was no communication since. He had friends who helped. My sister doesn't talk much about her inner life, but she does say that helping him die is the hardest thing she's ever done.

A commonplace thing about suffering: It brings us closer to God. Humbles us. Forty years in the desert as the model. Crucifixion as the model. Somewhere we get the idea that when things go well, we get to take credit. Suffering helps correct that.

My sister's Jim was a big guy like Ed. Liked Mexican food. We shared that. Lovely sense of humor. Drove a motorcycle when the weather was compatible. From Indiana but found his home in the Bay area. Once he and Nancy moved there—ten or twelve years ago—that's where he wanted to be.

I'm thinking God wanted to bring Jim closer to Him also through his suffering, but I don't know. I know I pray more now for both Jim and Nancy than I did before his illness. I don't think I prayed for him at all before his illness. In that way, I have drawn closer to Jesus as a result of Jim's suffering and death.

But suffering may happen also because we live in a universe of random processes, probabilistic processes. Because we have free will. These are God's inventions and He is active in them, but our will and natural law enter in as well. God isn't the only actor in the drama of cosmic events; he has also hired both us and the natural world to play our parts as well.

It's as if God as author has placed his surrogates into a play, let's say. A play that is a cross between science fiction, fantasy, journalistic realism, and internal monologue. Like any good, credible play (remember the phrase "willing suspension of disbelief" from high school English?), it is one in which the characters live lives independent from their author. He may influence them, but they—when a really good playwright is involved—will influence their creator equally. In fact, they will irritate, infuriate, frustrate, and generally drive their author to distraction because they will do what they want to do and not, generally, what their author would have them do.

The result of all this—natural law, free will, and God's active participation in the world—is that we experience both suffering and joy, the two masks on the face of creation.

I've known a few people to seek out suffering, who believe this is good for them. Builds character or something. But God isn't looking for gratuitous self-sacrifice from us. He isn't asking us to seek out opportunities to suffer, if the Gospel is our guide. If the Holy Spirit is our guide. In the Gospels, Jesus tries to alleviate the suffering of others, not to bring about His own. He endures suffering at the hands of an evil world because He is faithful to Abba Father. Because he does what God asks of Him.

Natural law, a probabilistic universe, and a general hostility toward Christians will bring suffering our way, sooner or later, and Jesus will come to meet us in that genuine, world-imposed suffering. That suffering we can't avoid.

Another Home Fellowship. Ed shares that "A Mighty Fortress is Our God" is a hymn that can bring him to tears, and he nearly comes to that as he begins to explain the effect the hymn has on him. He stops because he does not want to cry just now. I think of "And Did Those Feet in Ancient Time" and "The Doxology," placing them along with the other. I've got some other favorites, but these three stick out. "The Doxology" is the one my spine usually tingles—has tingled for decades—on, whether a self-proclaimed Christian, agnostic, atheist, or pagan. Whatever phase I've been in hasn't mattered. God has regularly tapped me on my shoulder and taken me in His arms on that particular song.

Ed can't understand why others find hymns boring and prefer praise music. We discuss the heavy plodding nature of most hymns, the blasting quality when they are played on cathedral organs, even modest church organs. Versus the gentle, accessible, light, folksy, unpretentious air in praise music. Well, Ed doesn't see it that way, or hear it, rather.

He likes the grand quality to hymns, I think. The drama of them. The heightened sense they bring to worship, the sense that all of this is of great moment. And he likes the emotional range of them, the extreme reach and risk of them.

But I like praise music too and perhaps because it is not heightened, not greatly dramatic, because in some sense it is the antithesis of all that. Plain music for plain folks. Just us here singing with our guitars and drums. Separate from institutions, the worship style not requiring the taxation wealth obtainable only by the Church or State—the instruments modest, inexpensive, the places of worship the very opposite of cathedrals. A feeling that this is more like the way the first century Christians worshipped and because of that, the music more genuine. Or having the greater potential for being genuine. Not as much put on. Puffed up. Self-conscious.

Another Home Fellowship. Ed wonders about the future of our church. The church leaders who appear to think of the Bible as a curiosity, an intellectual puzzle, a cultural document, a set of interesting stories. Not as history or as the revealed Word of God.

He wonders about the great numbers in our church who haven't yet accommodated themselves to women ministers and may never. Wonders about the storm over the proposed ordination of homosexuals and how that will come out. Wonders why it is that our church seems the eager adopter of new fashions and practices. Why there is little patience or accommodation accorded the conservatives among us. Feels like a lot of people have been left standing in a ditch as the enlightened church has moved into the fast lanes of the world.

# Elaine

Her home in which we meet. By her leave and her belief that we worship here.

Grandmother now. Several times over. Early to mid sixties. Used to be skinny as a rail, she says, and I believe it. Now she's got a little to her, some gravity. Not fat, by any means. Thin but muscular. Enough flesh to be interesting.

Tendons about her neck like a dozen strands of piano wire and nylon cord anchoring head to body, mind to matter. Her strength maintained by lifting coffee and coffee supplies for businesses, supporting her daughter. Carting this stuff from delivery vehicle up to break rooms all over town. Might as well lift at the Y a couple hours a day. Enjoys herself. Meets people all day long. Jokes. Howdies them.

Stops. Chats. Otherwise she'd just be bored to tears, she says. Presses the flesh and fathoms the spirit as she pumps the coffee.

Five children. Two adopted. Two in town. The rest, out.

At church, she often cries by the end of the service. So a box of tissues is in her area.

Has the genius of being original.

Third Sunday at church, perhaps, says, "Bill, come to our home fellowship. It's every Tuesday night, seven thirty. Close to you. Right downtown. Take the interstate to Myrrh. Here's a piece of paper."

She slows long enough for me to get a pen out and start writing.

"Interstate to Myrrh. You go east on Myrrh to Murphy. Myrrh deadends there. Turn right on Murphy. Go about five blocks. It's on the right. You can't miss it.

"We really need another man. There are just too many of us women. The food is always good. We keep ourselves well fed, you know. You'll like it. We'd love to have you. You'd balance us out, you know."

"Interstate to Myrrh," I said. "East on Myrrh, to what?"

"Murphy. It stops there. Have to go either right or left. Turn right. Several blocks down on the right, just after Greenglade. Near the corner of Greenglade. Can't miss it."

"What should I bring?"

"Just bring yourself. And a Bible, if you want. And a prayer book. Barclay's explaining the prayer book. But if you forget it or something, it doesn't matter. We'll have plenty there. Just bring yourself. You can manage that, can't you?"

"What?"

"To bring yourself. Ha, ha, ha."

"I think so." Of course. Enter into the home of strangers? Meet with a group of strangers in a strange home to do what? Talk about the Bible, a book I haven't read in decades, except for the past couple of months?

To talk about God, whom I haven't talked about in the context of belief for thirty-five years? To pray, which except for my recent solitary attempts in my Florida apartment I haven't any idea how to do, any idiom for. In fact, I have no prayer book and have to order one. It arrives a day before my first Home Fellowship meeting, just in time.

But I need it. I need this red-headed sixty-some year-old and her lanky, silver-haired, friendly, smiling, energetic, deliberate husband. I don't know exactly what "it" is at the

91

time, but I have an idea that comes close enough to provide guidance. That's why I say, "I think so." The idea I get from her and Billy and maybe a little bit from Jim chatting after a couple of services is what gets me going.

I don't know these people yet, but I need what they have. Whatever that is.

I know where my home is. My wife and children are in Indiana. I have an apartment in Florida. When I speak about going home, it's one place or the other. I know that much. I know my home is not in Maine, for example, or Arizona. Or at Jim and Elaine's. I know what I need isn't a home, because I have that. I have two of them, after all. I have an abundance of homes.

Anyway, it's a bright, summer Florida Sunday, and I say, "I think so." And that's that. Elaine has decided for me as I write her directions in a blank space on one of the flyers she has on her welcome desk in the entry to the breezeway to the church I'd come to by looking in a telephone book.

A church of about two hundred people all together, counting all the little ones, in a small stand of thin pines on a busy road whose altar stands against a soaring wall made up in large part, delightfully, of windows. Whose side walls are also windows for thirty feet or so from the altar wall back into the sanctuary. So that as one worships one may regard the effect of the breezes upon the trees and the color of the high, hopeful, Florida sky.

High windows, one might say, for a high prospect. No stained glass here. Clear as spring water to look out through into the deep. A deep one learns to regard—I learned to regard—as a child, summers, lying back in the backyard grass, nothing particular to do except look out into the blue, filling one's eyes with that color, filling one's mind. A simple opening of oneself to that immenseness, that great outer blue that appears to go on forever and on cloudless days comes down to a height just above the trees, far enough down so you think you can almost touch it.

And that, of course, is another sense of home. A home that can extend outward from a stretch of grass into the wide sky and beyond its blue illusion into the sparkling black on a summer day. A sense that one's being may easily stretch that far and still be home. Or that one's being may stretch itself far away into an imagined but actual interstellar space and still also then simultaneously reach back home to sense the backyard grass tickling the naked neck and thighs resting deep into its deep spikiness and smoothness.

And then the running of one's fingers over the grass, the tickling in one's fingers, the brush-cut grass. The cool feeling of the earth against one's back and buttocks and legs, the great firmness of it, in contrast to the warm, liquid air. The smell of the grass and the earth, the smell of fallen apples and fallen pears and ripe black raspberries and grapes and currents and gooseberries, a sweet, musky drink of smells and flavors in one's nose and mouth.

The feeling that the whole earth rounds itself around one and under one and holds one up and delights one intentionally, purposefully. As if this is where one belonged and belonged. As if this is the place one had longed for and now has and will keep, no matter what, wherever one may go afterward. But for the moment—a great long moment—one goes nowhere. Absolutely nowhere. Except all the places one can get to by lying just there. A moment that from time to time lasts hours as one drifts in and out of consciousness, is lost, found, lost, found, lost, found, lost, and found again in all that blue.

And so in my going to the church and worshipping for the first stretch of time in thirty-five years and as I let go my apprehension about sitting around with a lot of strangers marking one another with holy oil, talking about sprinkling Jesus' blood about on the brokenness and sorrow of the world, I begin to recover the way I saw the world when I was young. Particularly as I stand worshipping and singing, Sundays, looking out through trees, into the blue deep, as I again move out into it and it moves down into me.

"I think so," I say, as the bright sun lights our wide day, warms us, photonically enfolds us, enlivens us, however slightly lifting us up off our heels, shifting our bones and ligaments, our muscles and sinews forward in our frames, these organic devices we call ourselves, these sentient instrumentalities, these vessels, this machinery of our being, substratum of our dreaming, these word factories, these environmental mediation systems, these sensory translators, these information processing units, these mass storage devices, these globs of animated star stuff, these bundles of algorithms made flesh, these stones laid one on another, these casements opening onto prospects as varied as the cosmos, these idea machines, these dreams, these actors, these dreamers, these congresses, these primary residences, these geometers, these manifold recapitulating beneficiaries, these explorations of design space, these black boxes, these wholly-owned subsidiaries, these metronomes, these featherless bipeds, these speculative instruments, these loud silences, these polymaths, these possibilities, these metaphors.

Elaine's house is in the city, just south of downtown. Pleasant street of clapboard houses. None of that rundown sense you get in most urban neighborhoods in America. This is the old idea of what a city is. Should be. Well kept homes, yards. Not severely well kept up. Just moderately well. Well enough that one is pleased, but not so well that one worries for the spiritual well being of the people there. Slow cars. An occasional person strolling, two.

Elaine's and Jim's house, I should say. They both belong here. Both here by choice. Jazz clubs. Dining. Museums.

Symphonies. Operas. Theater. The city life is how they belong, where they've come to be who they are.

House is two stories. Front small porch. Wood floors. Kitchen, dining room, living room, sitting room, bathroom, enclosed area—Florida room—off the back that seems to have been a porch, then a porch off the back big enough to contain a large grill and space to pace if one has a mind to. Up, few bedrooms and a bath. Avocado tree in the back. This year, just one fruit as large as a melon.

Elaine prays like this: "Lord, I just hope You can do something to help Bill's wife, Pat. Her foot is painful to her, and I wish You would make that better so that she can go for her walks again, which she enjoys so much. And I wish You would also help Bill's daughter Katharine who is being teased about being thin. Help her, Lord, to see that being thin is not a bad thing and that what her tormentors say doesn't matter and that You love her, Lord, just as she is. Please help her to understand that she is pleasing to You just as she is and that this is what is really important. And I would like You to help Bill alone there in his apartment, also, to know that You love him and are taking care of his family up there in Indiana while he is separated from them in his new job. I ask these things in Jesus' name."

Prays with her eyes open.

One night, during prayer request time, Barclay asks for prayer for a client of his. I'll call her Mary. He's a psychotherapist, and she is the daughter of missionaries who abused her. According to Barclay, she has about as many things wrong with her as a person can have wrong. Number of major surgeries: She stopped counting at seventeen. Can't drive. Can't work. No family. Then he mentions her a second time at the next Home Fellowship.

Then Elaine goes into action. Late fall. Thanksgiving coming up. Gets Barclay to give her Mary's contact information, which she emails to everyone. Then she starts driving her around, trading off with the other women in the group. Once a week she schedules a few hours to do whatever Mary wants. Others too.

Barclay grins. Moony. Big. Round-faced. Soul-light streaming out at a megawatt. When Elaine or Minnie or Twila speak about what they do together with Mary. Where they go.

Pleased. Usually pleased. A comedy always in progress beneath the words and expressions and gestures. Sometimes deep. Others, right there on the surface.

"I just can't help myself, Bill," she says one night. "I just buy things. This thing. That thing. Oh, you know. Whatever. Whatever cries out the loudest to me.

"You didn't know that, did you? That I can hear the voices of retail items. It's true. I really do. And God has told me to liberate them. To bring them home where I can care for them.

"It's a burden. Really it is. The way they cry so pathetically. You don't know. You laugh. But think of them: knick-knacks, bric-a-brac, vases, crockery of all sorts, pictures, whatever. Treated so insensitively by sales clerks, so impersonally.

"And think of poor Jim. Slaving away day and night to put two nickels together in his pocket. And here I am liberating his nickels too. Reaching right in there and circulating them.

"You know, money only does people good in circulation. And boy am I a good circulator. I just keep those nickels spinning, don't I Jim?"

Mother. Grandmother. Watches her grandchildren regularly. Every week, a few days.

Meets with an accountability group—several women from the church—one day a week.

Study groups for women who are interested in what Christianity is all about or maybe want to get past the basics to the caviar and pheasant under glass. Once a week for six or eight or ten or twelve weeks, depending.

Welcome committee. Or at least used to. Or sometimes still does. Stands at a table at the entryway to the church and engages everyone but especially new people. Friends gather, coming and going, helping her greet new people. Greets me on my first day.

Clearinghouse. Email central for prayer requests for an outsized group of friends, former Home Fellowship members, and acquaintances. Central terminus and distribution point for news and prayers and well-wishing.

Then a night at the Home Fellowship: "He won't let anything go. Anything. When someone does something, he has to say yes or no.

"There's an inner circle, and then there's the rest of us. I don't understand. You'd like to have something you can do that is yours to do. Know what I mean?

"Well, I shouldn't be talking about him this way, especially with a new person here. Bill, I'm sorry. But I'm just upset. What makes him think treating people badly is okay?

"He's a wonderful teacher. We are blessed that way. I've learned a lot from him. But I like to be liked, you know? Who doesn't? But he makes you feel. I don't know."

Barclay laughs. "Different people have different gifts."

"What do you mean, Barclay?"

"Some ministers have a pastoral gift. Others have a gift for teaching. I've never met anyone with both."

"But you'd think a pastor would have a better . . . ." Barclay laughs again. Shakes his head.

"Sometimes it's just very difficult," she says.

Elaine's father died not too long ago. Elaine and Jim take care of Elaine's mother, attend the funeral. "There were people there we hadn't seen in thirty-two years," she says. "Most of the great-grand-children were there, and everyone said how well-behaved they were.

"We had the funeral in the church rather than the funeral home. I praise the Lord for that. It was the church they'd gone to for many years. Many family friends. They stopped going there when we—Jim and I—had some trouble there. A disagreement. It had to do with gifts of the Spirit. Anyway, we left, and Mother and Daddy left too. So it was good after all these years to return there and to still feel loved by those good people. To see them again.

"We're still getting cards and letters saying how wonderful it was to get together and see everyone. Too bad Daddy wasn't there to enjoy it."

"But don't you think he might have been?" Kathy asks.

"I attended a funeral once—it was my grandmother—where I couldn't pay any attention to the service because she was right there. I mean I couldn't see her. But I had this overwhelming feeling she was standing right there over by the tree." Anne Marie waves her hands around like Vanna White, indicating the baffling and extraordinary presence of her aunt down at the end of the couch, where Twila is sitting.

"You don't think God lets those who have passed attend their own funerals?" asks Billy, skeptical, as though he were talking about a person's birthday. A person attending his own birthday party.

"Whatever," Elaine replies, a fixed look to her eyes, as though she is watching something none of the rest of us can see.

"It couldn't have gone better. We kept Mother busy. She had her family and friends around her. And I've been okay except for a week ago tomorrow. It was my first day back from all of it, and it was just a terrible day. I hope I don't have any more like that."

"Well, you know," Kathy says, "don't you think he's gone on to his real life? His actual life that this is a preparation for?

"I had a friend who had Lou Gerhig's disease. Her body just gradually failed her, gradually stopped working. And when that was done, she died. And the way God helped me to understand that was that He had now given her her real body and that she was now living her real life with Him."

Her real life with Him. The afterlife. Immortality. All a new Christian like me can do initially is file this away. I mean I've had it in my head I would disappear and turn to dust for so long, it isn't going away any time soon. The idea of cessation. A dreamless sleep.

Heaven. What it means, I have no idea. How to think about my terrestrial life in the context of infinite continuation elsewhere isn't clear. Oh yes, I've read *The Great Divorce*. In theory, it seems right, but who knows? All I know for sure is that the present has become momentous as a result. Dramatically imbued. Potent with possibility. Or one might think of it like a stand-up comedy routine. Each of us, on the spot. The comedian. What joke we tell and how we tell it makes all the difference.

Later, by several months, I am speaking with Ken, my family God expert. Near his home in Michigan. Land of clouds and rain, where I grew up. We are speaking about suffering. The problem of suffering for Christians and for those who are considering becoming Christians. Pain and suffering. Why God would allow the horrible things to happen to His children that in fact do happen to them every day. He points out a family leaving church that morning who have just lost their two-month-old baby a few days before, and it is Mother's Day. What a Mother's

Day for that young woman. The funeral flowers are still in the sanctuary on Sunday.

And as we are driving together down Washtenaw Avenue in Ann Arbor, it occurs to me that Heaven makes it work. Something about heaven. If you could actually have a conversation with someone on the other side who had suffered horribly, you might find that they are easy about it. That they would feel about it the way an adult might feel about a bad dream he experienced in childhood, decades ago. Yes, the person on the other side might say, it was not pleasant as it was happening, but it's over now, and it really wasn't so bad.

Well, that's what Ken and I come to one day. Yes, there are many chains of reasoning Christians have come up with to understand pain and suffering. But this one seems to explain the most with the least. For me, anyways. An eternity in heaven for a bit of suffering preparation down here, suffering like a child suffers learning his ABCs. Medieval, one might think. Or maybe more accurately, first century.

Oh, I know. It doesn't quite wash. But I think that may be because of our parochial perspective. Parochial. Timebound. Once we have an opportunity to step outside this particular corner of the cosmos and to extract time's arrow from our hearts, we will know such things differently. And they will make sense.

Sometimes I think those who suffer the most here will be the most blessed in Heaven. There is evidence for this in the Gospels, in what Jesus says about the rich and the poor.

But however it works out, I'm certain it will be just. Because we are assured by Jesus that the Father is just.

Message from Elaine on my apartment answering machine, 7:30 A.M. Wednesday, some months ago: "Bill, I just woke up this morning convicted that I'd offended you, and I want to apologize. I just got going last night, cutting up and whatever, and I didn't think. I mean, I wasn't thinking. About the sexual innuendos or whatever. You are a good Christian man, and we love you and respect you, and I want you to know how much we value you in our Home Fellowship, and I want you to know I'm going to try very hard not to make comments like that again. I just wanted you to know. I apologize."

That Wednesday night, I play it twice. Try calling her a couple times, but she isn't home.

Message from me on Elaine's home answering machine, 8:00 A.M. Thursday: "Elaine, no offense taken, really. Nothing. You didn't do anything out of line or anything. Nothing to apologize for. Sometimes. I don't know. I get shy or embarrassed or something. I don't understand it. But you weren't out of line at all. I very much enjoy your Home Fellowship, and I look forward to it a great deal."

Message from Elaine on my apartment answering machine, Thursday afternoon: "Thank you, Bill."

Another Home Fellowship. I bring the food. Jim says, when I arrive, he and Elaine wondered whether I remembered it was my turn to bring the food. Well certainly. Next day, Elaine emails me with thanks for the meal: "Thank you so very much for the absolutely delicious dinner you prepared for us Tuesday evening. You sure outdid yourself, and we all appreciated it a lot."

Another Home Fellowship. In advance, by email, she asks me to speak about how I came to follow the Way. It is part of an exchange in which she again thanks me for a meal I cooked. Two days on and off to prepare. Great northern beans, garlic, carrots, onions, pork, beef, Cornish hens, lamb, thyme, pepper sauce, salt, pepper, parsley, and some other stuff. A stew, really. A kind of *cassoulet*. Not a *vrai cassoulet*, maybe, but an Elkington *cassoulet*, certainly.

In a return message, I tell her how my idea of heaven is having my own restaurant in which I get to prepare and serve my favorite dishes to all my family and friends. And I thank her and Jim for opening their home to me, for their generosity, Christian tutelage, their excellent example, patience, and so forth for someone learning again to be a Christian.

At the meeting, I am a bit sweaty as we gather, get our drinks, help Barclay prepare the food, move chairs around, say our hellos. Drink in my case usually means some herbal tea. Others have cokes or wine or coffee. Barclay has a mess of sea trout that he and his guide have caught. Taken from the ocean. Baked in foil on the grill with garlic butter, salt, and pepper. Salad with Feta cheese crumbled in, Greek olives, mild peppers from a jar, onions, romaine. Garlic bread.

Lovely meal, but as I say, I am a little sweaty thinking about telling my story, giving my testimony. Testimony. Sounds a little like one is on trial or something. Before and during dinner comments like, don't hold anything back now. Make sure you tell us all the juicy details. Don't leave anything out.

Then Barclay sits out back after the meal smoking his cigar and drinking coffee with cream and sugar. I stay out with him as the others wait for us. Elaine comes out and sits with us. Reminds us that I am the entertainment and that the time for the entertainment has arrived. So we go in, gather in the living room.

Robert and Lucy, two new members who meet with us for the first time that night: Friends of Barclay who go a long way back. Jim and Elaine. Twila. Kathy. Scotty. Kim. The rest are out of town or busy.

Twila shares about how Travis, her husband, a non-Believer at present, corrected their son at dinner the other night, in the way he offers grace. He tosses it off, no sincere emotion. Quick and dirty. No, you need to respect your mother and God, he says. It's Mother's Day. You're talking to God. Try it again.

"Anyone else?" Jim asks.

Then she shares about how Michael has been acting out at school and at home and how she prays over him with others and how his attitude changes completely after that.

"Anyone else before we turn it over to Bill?" Jim asks.

Then Kathy shares about how she is sending letters out to a number of the members of the group asking for financial support for her work. Her work involves international evangelism, and she is expected to get contributors to support her salary and the costs of her work, such as travel, supplies, overhead, support people, lights and facilities apportioned on a per person basis, and so forth. Her face is a little flushed as she begins to speak. It is the most difficult part of her work, she says, but most of the staff in her organization are funded this way, including its president.

"Anyone else want to share before we turn it over to Bill?"

Twila shares about how she is thinking of joining a singing group. One of the previous members of the group whose behavior and speech were objectionable was asked to leave, and that cleared the way for her to seriously consider joining it. There is a time commitment issue. She has to be away from home, on the road, performing, some amount of the time. Travis needs to be supportive. She plans to broach the subject at dinner Thursday night, a night out for the two of them.

All of this is quite interesting, but meanwhile my palms are a little clammy as I sip my second cup of tea, looking forward to its calming effects. While I am getting the tea, Lucy moves so that I can sit where everyone can see me. So I sit there out in the open, flapping in the breeze as the others share and my moment approaches.

"Anyone else?" Jim asks. No one speaks up.

After waiting about ten seconds—which is really more like minutes in such circumstances—Jim says, "Bill has agreed to tell us his story tonight. So Bill, why don't you go ahead?"

I clear my throat. I clear it again. Someone asks if I would change my seat so that everybody can see me. So I do. People move away as if they're going to get a show or something, a little space between them and me. A chair away.

So here I am separated off. Wondering what I should say. What I shouldn't say. Then I just start talking.

"I'll try to make a long story short. Don't want to bore anybody.

"I was raised a Christian in a somewhat casual household, somewhat casual about God and its beliefs about God.

I went to church many Sundays, but not all, and that was about it.

"Then I went away to boarding school and went to chapel six days a week. Required. Compulsive worship didn't go over well with me. Compulsive belief.

"Also, God couldn't possibly exist with all the suffering in the world back then. The war—the Viet Nam War—and murder and torture and starvation and disease. Not only the 20th century but every other century I'd read about.

"I wasn't what you'd call a joyous child. Morose maybe. Church people seemed to me to be superficial or out of it or hypocritical. Most adults seemed that way. Their credibility on Christianity pretty close to zero.

"Oh, there were developmental issues, but that's how I thought.

"Jesus seemed holy. But I couldn't make that make sense with everything else.

"Then there was a long period of just sort of, we are organisms that somehow got here operating on certain discoverable principles. Evolved here, probably. Developed out of the ooze like everything else. Just coasting along like that.

"Fell in love. Got married. Pat agreed: Too much suffering in the world for God to exist. A nurse sees patients die, and she saw her share.

"Took to drinking. Liked it. Drank more. Drank pretty heavily for a number of years. Pretty unhappy.

"Had kids. Lovely stuff. Best thing we ever did.

"Still kept drinking. Pat objected on and off. Then forced the issue. Told me to back off or else. I did back off, but I didn't quit. Then I got picked up for DWI. DUI. Whatever they call it. Arrested. Thrown into jail for the better part of a night. Had a choice, either get counseling and education or go back to jail for a couple of months. Chose the counseling.

"What the counselors said made sense. I read some of the AA literature. *The Big Book.* Some of the other stuff. About two thirds through I figured I was an alcoholic. I didn't drink every day. Pretty much only on weekends. Not every weekend. Infrequently on weekends. But it was clear. That's what I was. Am. I craved a drink from time to time. You know when you crave a drink, there's something wrong.

"So. I quit. Enough of that. I felt lousy. Who needs to feel like that, anyway? So I stopped. Started reading the Bible. The AA people stress the importance of the spiritual angle; so I thought I'd try to understand that. Delved into it in hotel rooms on business trips. The Gideons.

"Next thing I know Nate's a Christian. Seems to change him for the better. He feels better about things. I feel better about things. I read the Bible a little more. King James, mainly.

"Then I move here, leave Pat and Nate and Katharine back home. Come here for a job. Leave them there so Nate can finish high school with his friends. Commute back every few weeks. Then last summer, Pat and Katharine come to visit. Pat brings a book. *The Case for Christ.* Strobel. Lee Strobel. The reasons Christianity makes sense. The evidence. The logic. Apologetics for the layman. Said Nate had asked her to read it. Me. So I read it in the week and a half they are visiting.

"Oh, maybe they leave, and I finish it the next day. Something like that. By the end of it, I'm wondering where I can get a Bible, and I'm flipping through the Yellow Pages under 'Churches.' (I left King James at home.)

"The evidence and logic are very strong. Evidence and logic for the miracles, the resurrection. The signs Jesus is God.

So good, so strong, I was left wondering what my problem had been. Trying to remember. Couldn't. Thought I'd better get on with it.

"So that's that.

"I tried one other church before I stopped by ours. Didn't like what the pastor had to say. Talked to Ken, my brother-in-law. He suggested the denomination of the church I grew up in. So I looked for one in the area where I wanted to buy a house.

"So that's that. That's how it came about."

Then I want to tell about something else that happened, but I don't. I don't know why. Shy. Cowardly, perhaps. Here is what I didn't say then: "Then one Sunday at church, Mark asked those who felt a special need for prayer to come up to the altar. Irregular. Provoked I think by that itinerant prophet who used to come by, what he said that day. I forget what it was. Anyway I went up.

"There were maybe eight or ten of us kneeling at the altar. He asked me what's on my mind. I started blubbering something about how I just hope everything will work out at my new job. Tears streaming down. Hadn't cried in decades. Felt weird. The Holy Spirit. And he gave me a look like right, this is about a job. Then he asked if I have accepted Jesus as my personal savior. Asked me to repeat a bunch of stuff after him that says that I accept Jesus Christ as my personal savior. I forget what it is exactly. I repeat it."

I wish I could, but I don't.

"And that, as I say, is that. How I became a Christian."

Well, after that Elaine thanks me and various thank me, and I'm happy it's over.

One asks God for help in such things, but one inevitably feels one is somewhat on one's own. One doesn't know exactly what to say and what not to say. One wants to be honest, but one doesn't really want to dig in the dirt, because digging in the dirt and flinging all that dirt around gets everyone to feeling a little dirty.

One wants to call a spade a spade and move onto the next implement.

Another Home Fellowship. Elaine says she just needs to share that she said something that offended one of us a few weeks before and that she's sorry and that after she learned about it she sent a letter to the person who took offense and apologized. She didn't mean anything. She was just talking, and maybe she wasn't thinking or paying attention or as much attention as she should have been paying, and she would try to not do that again. She certainly doesn't want to offend nor does she intend to offend or be mean or be inconsiderate. And if she had it to do over again of course she wouldn't say anything. And she says she doesn't know what more she can do except to say she's sorry.

Jim smiles and looks over at me as she's speaking and says something like, "Well I'm sure nothing like this has ever happened to you before."

"Well, I surely hope it doesn't happen again," she says in response. "This has been terrible."

"Well, if you've apologized, what more can you do?" someone says.

"We're taught that we should ask forgiveness. You've done that. Now it's up to the other person," someone else contributes.

"I'm just not going to talk anymore," Elaine says. "That way I'll be sure I don't say anything anyone will have a problem with. I mean, I know what I said was wrong. Otherwise, there wouldn't be a problem. But I had no idea at the time that I was saying anything anybody would, you know, have a problem with. It just seemed normal.

"But that's enough of that. I'm just not going to talk any more at Home Fellowship. Or anywhere. I'll just sit here and listen to you all and mind my own business."

Alpha Small Group. We're sharing in the small group part of the Alpha course, a course on Christianity that Kathy, Elaine, Jim, and I are helping with, and Elaine says, "I was leading my study group. You know. The Friday morning thing. A few of us women get together. And I was telling a few of them. We'd come to the end of the study. About how God doesn't want us to worry. How, in fact it's a sin to worry, to be anxious about anything. You see, it takes our minds off of God, and it shows that we don't trust him to work things out. Worry and anxiety. Whether it's about money or children or whatever, you know. The Bible teaches us to turn all that over to God. To put our lives in his hands. To do our best and then just forget it. Move on. Leave the rest to Him.

"And He is faithful, you know. I mean, I believe completely in journaling. In keeping a journal or diary or whatever you call it. You just write in there whatever you like, whatever you are thinking. I keep it beside me in the morning during my devotions. Sometimes keep it with me all day. And I write in there the prayers I pray for. And I write in there when my prayers and others' prayers are answered. And then I can look back whether it's a day or a month or a year. And I can see how faithful He is.

"It's true. He is faithful. And we shouldn't worry, because He is faithful. It's easy to forget. I don't know what it is about us, but we so easily forget what we've prayed for. We forget that our prayers have been answered. And when we forget we wonder where God is, why he is so distant. Sometimes we wonder whether He exists. But then if you have your journal, you can read back over all the things He's done and see how faithful He has been."

Then Kathy says, "Yes. Sometimes we think, this is too weird. This Biblical stuff, you know. Sometimes we think, this is science fiction. This stuff about the virgin birth. Someone's made this up. And I've just made this up, too. There's just this group of us that must be hallucinating or something. But then you look at what God does in your life and the lives of others you know. You see Him bringing things about that are absolutely amazing, unpredictable because they are so weird. So improbable. So good. But He does these kinds of things every day. His faithfulness is thorough and incomprehensible.

"Like Elaine says, we forget. There's something in us that makes us forget how good He has been to us. So we need to remind ourselves. I know I do. And I've been keeping a journal as well, and I'm always surprised and amazed when I read back over it and recognize all the things He's done."

Another Alpha Small Group. We're sharing, and Elaine talks about the remarkable things God does: "I think it was the Gospel Businessmen's Association. Thousands of people. Some speaker. Some speaker I don't even know, didn't know then either. And what's his name, Jim? That man you didn't like?"

"What man?"

"That man you couldn't stand, or something. I forget his name. The used car salesman, I think he was. Wasn't he?"

"I don't know what you're talking about."

"Well, never mind, then. I think he was a used car salesman. And I don't care whether he did lay hands on me. He could have done anything to me, and it would have been fine because of what he did.

"Anyway, I was scared. Frightened. Just fearful, and I couldn't shake it, you know. It just got hold of me when Jim was away. Came over me so even in the hot weather, summer, and no air conditioning, I would close all the windows in the house I was so scared.

"Who knows what might have happened. If I'd kept that up. That fear.

"Anyway, this man comes walking down the isle and spots me. He's looking, and I don't know what he's looking at, except he's looking at me. Right at me. Bold, you know. Like that. Then he says, 'Young woman. You have the spirit of fear in you. Don't you?'

"'Well, yes,' I said. And he grabbed me by the shoulders. Rough. A little rough, maybe, but I don't care. And then he prays for the spirit of fear to leave me. And it did. It just did. And it hasn't ever returned."

"I remember now," Jim says.

"I thought you would. And you were upset."

"Oh, I don't know."

"Yes, you were. You didn't like that man touching your young wife was all. But isn't it amazing how God uses us? How he can change our lives just like that?"

# Jim

Jumps up and down. Hops like someone on a pogo stick. TV's on. Florida room. Basketball. He stands six-five, six-six maybe. Gray. Fit. Runs everyday. Lanky. Sound's off. Second overtime. Thick hair bounces, ripples like a grizzly's pelt.

Rest of us Brownian about as Minnie glides the food out. Barclay and I speak about Fredrick Buechner, whom he has not read. He reads psychotherapy books and books like *Hunt for Red October*. Stays away from Christian literature. Work reading. Escape. Bible goes without saying.

Quiet. Not even throat noises. Driving up from the toes and balls of his feet. Played basketball competitively in various amateur leagues until he was 57. Hair bristles up as if he would charge.

Another night, he tells of a coworker—Darren—who visits the Fellowship several times in my short time. Wife tells him she wants a separation. One day shortly after this, Darren is visiting with patients in the hospital he works in with Jim, discovers a patient—a Christian woman—who reads him a Psalm. Darren shares his marriage difficulties with her. She prays for God's healing, for God to drive the evil one from his marriage, cussing Satan to the ends of the echoing white hospital hallways. That same day, with no prodding from him, Darren's wife tells him she does not want a separation after all, and Jim's throat catches for a moment in the telling, his eyes a little watery, then he goes on to the end, smiling and grateful for God's hand in it.

Another night, he asks for prayer concerning his job. His annual review is the next day. Not much to do these days. He's delegated it all. Would like to work another year or two. Would like an interesting assignment. Next meeting, the review goes well. Much bigger bonus than he thought. Still not clear what he will be assigned to, but he's confident, and we pray for him and his manager to receive guidance.

When Geoffrey, his grandson, comes over to visit, he grins big as an orthodontist's ad, picks him up, hugs him, takes him over to his new toy box, catches the ball that Geoffrey pulls out and slings, remarkably hard, at a difficult angle in Jim's direction. Fast hand snags it.

Leads us in singing. Leads us in prayer. Leads us in sharing. Will lead us in Bible study when others don't. Solid teaching, always. The decades of humble study in the way his hands thumb through, the way his voice courses over the words, familiar to him as the furnishings of his home. The group's biggest eater. Truly appreciates food. Mass quantities of the best stuff. You know you are a hit, when he goes back for thirds. Seconds may simply mean a caloric deficit that needs repayment.

Takes five in his Florida room after our meal as the women gather about Elaine at the dining room table, chatting about menstruation and breast feeding and taking care of difficult sons and daughters and moving and marrying and ovarian irregularities and hysterectomies and mammograms and giving birth and gift-giving and worshipping and jobs and parents and the difficulties and technicalities and curiosities of all these things.

Chairman of the board of a local theater group. On the board of a downtown revitalization group. Church leader. Sunday school teacher. Junior Achievement instructor. Former bassist in amateur jazz ensembles; his bass rests in the corner of the living room.

Drives a red Mercedes. Runs quiet. A little awkward, perhaps because of his height. But smooth when he brings Christ to another. Angles him in, straight to the heart.

I tell Jim about a disagreement—a dispute, really—between me and my son. Evolution versus Creationism. Perturbed. That particular night for some reason. Still distracts. The idea that he (one, I should say) can simply ignore the evidence. Wish it away. But there's Jim calmly saying, "But is this a central issue? Is it significant?"

After that, on one of my infrequent trips home to Indiana, as Nate shows me a plastic license plate frame he's bought that shows a fish labeled "God" devouring another fish labeled "Darwin," I have to laugh with him. God swallows everything. All of us. Our ideas. No matter how meritorious or useful or clever or satisfying or explanatory or incisive or aesthetically pleasing or creative or logical or fashionable. Or silly or deluded or off the mark or unsubstantiated or evasive or doltish. Every thought begins in Him because thinking itself begins in him. He sorts them out through his children. Uses all of them. None of them complete. All partial, including this one.

He speaks all of it. He speaks all of us. And in His speaking, He reveals His will. And He will have us work out our way toward Him, step by step, word by word, work by work. And if that way is mistaken, oblique, indirect, it is indirect.

But of course all ways are indirect. Just as space is curved, so is God. The shortest distance between any two points in two dimensional space is a straight line, but we do not live in two dimensional space. The lines we follow meander, wobble, gyrate, tangle, come round upon themselves. Then veer off again.

We live inside a story of which God is the lead author and we are his collaborating writers. And as in any good novel or poem or play—any imaginative work— the unfolding, the revealing, the progress is by indirect means. By a wandering over a topography that is always new and often surprising and usually possesses a lot of up and down.

And just as He works out His story through us and we work out our stories through Him, so also is our understanding worked out in our relations with others. Other Christians and non-Christians. Our progress is revealed in our relations, our speaking with others and our speaking out of ourselves, our acts, our silences, in the net of meanings we make together that catch us up as any good net will catch and hold the things it is designed for.

And so it is in Elaine's and Jim's Home Fellowship. Stranger in a sandy state, separated from wife and daughter and son for weeks at a time on a new job. And here is Jim thrusting his hand down into the net and pulling out a truth I can't see about my son and me until he places it flopping and staring and thumping on the floor in front of me. But there it is. Here dine on this. It's real food. And it does sustain me as my son and I speak through to who we are together and who we will become, speak more Christ when we speak Christ, speak less an oceanic roil than an illumined underwater.

One meeting during sharing, he speaks about his wallet. His literal wallet. Before church, he runs up to a gas station to fill up. He and Elaine drive to church. He teaches Sunday school. Reaches for the wallet for some reason. Not there. Drives back over to the gas station. Looks all around. Drives back over to church. Speaks with Elaine at the end of the service. Leaves quickly thereafter, Elaine driving so that he can begin composing the list of cards that have been lost or taken. So that he can call them in.

On the way, Elaine prays. Asks God to allow her to find the wallet in her mailbox when they arrive home. When they get there, he looks inside. There. Lying open. Pulls it out. Wide-eyed. Not speechless but not talkative either. When they open the door, a note slipped under on the floor. A child's hand, almost. About how the person found it scattered down the street. Picked up everything in sight.

No name. No phone. Money. Cards. Everything appears to be there. Appears to be almost like it was.

Wide-eyed. Quiet. Breathing. Looking. These old Christians.

Another meeting. Sharing. This is maybe the sixth month. The time spins by like a flicked penny skittering across a table. He has insufficient work to do. Thinking about retirement but not ready. Not really. Has been told they want him to stay. But the assignments are thin. Sparse as Billy's hair. Someone suggests seminary. Jim holds his mouth carefully, not one line on his face changing.

Someone else says, "Maybe God's preparing you."

And: "Perhaps the Lord's trying to help you lean on Him more."

Jim smiles. Not clear. Think some more on this one. What's one to do? Ask for guidance. Pray. All of us. For help on this one.

Background. It's forty years ago Jim became a Christian. Accepted Jesus as his savior. Thirty-five years ago, he was baptized in the Holy Spirit. Spoke in tongues. Reserved. Reticent. This is the last thing he is interested in. But there it is one night. A meeting. He's prayed over, and it happens. Preacher that night says he will soon have a large positive effect on young people. He. Jim. A prophecy.

The next day, Jim leaves for a week supervising juvenile delinquents at a camp. On the last night of the camp, after a brief presentation from Jim on Jesus, many of the boys ask for help in becoming Christians. Jim and the rest of the counselors move from boy to boy all evening as they accept Jesus. And as he tells this, at thirty-five years' distance, Jim's eyes redden and become watery, and his voice clogs.

Early Home Fellowship. Speaking about the Bible. I've been reading it, really reading it, for the first time in centuries. Well, less, but not much. Been concentrating on the New Testament. Grave troubles with Paul. Deep doubts about how to understand him. Off-putting at least, his talk about the virtues of celibacy, about how he does not boast. Does not boast? Only that he has the personal authority of Jesus Christ. Without of course ever having followed Him when he was alive. Passes himself off as an expert on Christ when he never even meets the guy. And then all that visceral disgust with lust, apparently with homosexuality and extramarital sex and promiscuity.

My brother is a homosexual. He has lived in a committed relationship with another man for maybe a decade and a half. There's a great deal of respect, love, and care there. James, my brother, says he's a Christian. One takes him at his word.

How this should be regarded with great horror escapes me, when real sources of horror abound: children killing their parents, parents killing their children, parents sexually abusing their children, adults kidnapping, sexually abusing, and killing children, men kidnapping, sexually abusing women, and killing them. Greed is everywhere. Pride is everywhere. Cruelty is everywhere. These last three kinds of sins are considered virtues in many of their forms by most in the U.S. At work, they are largely encouraged or indulged. Here are sins worthy of real disgust, and they are certainly sins Jesus singles out as being particularly grievous.

But nowhere that I can find does Jesus discuss homosexuals or pre-marital sex. Adultery is clearly a sin. But Jesus doesn't go on and on about it. Let's stop doing this, he says, and moves on to the sins that most concern him.

So I have problems with Paul, and I say to Jim and to Barclay and the rest that I have problems with him. And Jim says, "I have problems with Paul too." That helps. That helps a lot. After Jim says this, it's easier being a Christian.

Many months later, I begin to imagine Paul's situation. Helping the non-Jews become Christians. Perhaps promiscuity of all kinds was the norm among them. How to get a handle on this fixation, this distraction, is his problem. Hyperbole might be part of the answer. Hyperbole. Overstatement to make a point. Like Jesus saying we must hate our father and mother, indeed must hate our own lives, must give up all our possessions to follow Him. Hate is a pretty strong word when it comes to parents. It would seem to contradict one of the Ten Commandments. Give up all our possessions. One would be reduced to nakedness. Is this literally what Jesus wants of us? To run around naked in the ice and the snow?

Another Home Fellowship. Jim reports on the meetings of the Magnificent Seven, the name that emerges for our pastor's kitchen cabinet, kitchen advisors. Mark is thinking about our congregation leaving the larger church. The real issue seems to be the ordination of homosexuals. This is being played out against a perception that the wider church leadership is drifting away from the authority of the Bible. Many wider church leaders believe it is an interesting historical document, full of legendary stories, but that it is not to be depended upon as a source of historical truth. I get this picture after many conversations over dinners stretching out a couple of months.

"Nothing's been decided," he says. "We're in a fact finding phase."

I speak with Susan in the kitchen. "Why are we so concerned about homosexuality?" I ask. "Jesus wasn't. He was concerned about pride and arrogance and cruelty and greed and self-interest and a dispirited, prideful attention to the law."

"I haven't heard anyone talk about the issue in those terms," she replies.

"Maybe they ought to read their Bibles," I say. I feel pretty good about it too, until I begin to feel the opposite about an hour or two later. Until I feel pretty silly about what I've said a day or two later. The outrageous pride there is in it. The sophomoric arrogance.

Another Home Fellowship. Jim hugs me, and that feels very good.

Another Home Fellowship. Talking about Iggy Pop. Ziggy Stardust. David Bowie. But Iggy Pop in particular. Iggy and the Stooges. Iggy falling on broken glass, shirtless, as part of the performance, part of the rock experience, back in the early days, back in his Detroit era. Jim overhears this conversation I'm having with Scotty and Twila and says Iggy was just in town, says in the paper Iggy is quoted as saying that he had been heavily influenced by jazz, especially by John Coltrane. "I can see that," I say.

"Do you like jazz," he asks.

"Yes I do."

"Do you like John Coltrane?"

"Yes I do. I especially like 'My Favorite Things.'"

"This is exciting."

"How so?"

"We may have hit upon something we can talk about."

Another Home Fellowship. His job has changed. He's taken a 20% cut. He used to be responsible for the operation of a hospital that has just now been fully incorporated into the operations of a larger medical center, and he is now one of a number of managers. "I'm satisfied," he says in a balanced sort of way. "I used to be responsible for a hospital, and I had the opportunity to do that for awhile, and that was good. But this is fine. I was worried I wouldn't have a job, once the integration was complete. So this situation is welcome.

"It isn't exactly clear what my new responsibilities will be, but I'm looking forward to helping to shape them. I'm sixty-six, and it isn't often these days that a man my age, in my situation, has the opportunity to stay on, to be given continued employment with a pretty good company. So I'm satisfied with it."

Kind of a sad look to him as he sits there talking. Lines deepen in his face. The eyes big and maybe a little more fluid than usual. The hands raspy as they rub together.

Another Home Fellowship. One of several in our August holiday. This night we meet at a café in a fashionable suburban town on a street with upscale shops, the asphalt tastefully replaced with brick. His granddaughter joins us for dinner, handsome young woman finishing up college about thirty miles from where Nate is just starting out. A Christian school, Pentecostal. Basketball player. Majoring in physical education. Wants to be a personal trainer. Fit. Strong. Full of good humor. The poise of Diana, The Huntress. Nothing will get in this young woman's way, at least not for long. A will there that would track anything to the ground.

Sits next to her grandfather, chatting with him, a family resemblance reflected between them in the cheekbones, the noses, as he appreciates his tall golden beer.

Another Home Fellowship. One of many in which, toward the end of the evening, his three-year-old blond-haired grandson flies in, latches on to him, and won't let go.

Prayer at church. Two days after Nine-Eleven, Jim and Elaine and Susan and I, along with about forty or fifty other adults attend a special prayer service for the victims and the terrorists. After the service, as I wait for Katharine and he for his grandson, who are in youth group, Jim and I discuss the terrorism in the breezeway, in the dark, mosquitoes biting as we slap. He mentions "Islamic extremists," and I recalled a fellow I heard on the radio, a Muslim, who said that the people who did this were not Muslim. They couldn't be. They were simply evil.

"Oh, they're Muslim alright," Jim says.

"If someone were to call himself a Christian and were to do what these people did, would you believe him to be Christian?" I ask.

"I'm not going to judge," Jim says. "I've known Muslims who would never have anything to do with something like this, and I've known others who are hotheads. Oh, I'm sure there are white supremacists who are just as bad as these guys, maybe worse."

John is there and Tim. The four of us standing around together waiting for kids. And even though we have just prayed in the sanctuary for blessings on our enemies and forgiveness for them, as we are taught, there arises among us talk of how we would eliminate terrorism. How our country might go about it. About military action that might be taken. About the fittingness of this. The reasonableness of that.

As I say, we are slapping mosquitoes in the dark, just waiting. Just talking. And I have the sense of how small we are and how dark everything is getting and how strange the world is and we are also. The sense that if one really pressed into any of the ideas we have or think we have or are trying to express that one would find dust and darkness. And maybe that is why we don't probe too deeply.

Well of course we don't have much time either. We have children to take home in a few minutes. How deeply can one probe into things before one must get in one's car and disappear down the road? How much room is there for such ideas when one's children seem to narrow one's life to a fanatic and busy love.

Alpha Group. Halloween night. Jim, Elaine, Blake, and Sandra. The rest—Pat, Bart, Connie, Spencer, and Carrie—all off doing Halloween things. Topic of Nicky Gumbel's talk on the tape tonight is discerning God's will for one's life through the Bible, common sense, advice from fellow Christians, visions and dreams, the touching of one's heart, and so forth. Jim's Alpha leader's book has suggestions in it about what questions to ask to get the conversation going. How do you feel about turning your life over to God, about seeking his guidance, or some such thing, is one.

I talk about how God has made clear to me that I am to be where I am, geographically and at work. How in the Home Fellowship we studied Brennan Manning's *The Signature of Jesus* and how something in it really hit home: How do you learn humility without humiliation? How I had in effect taken a demotion at work when I took the job that brought me to the area. How a few years ago I would have told my new company's management where to stick it. How I would have found another job, brushed the dust off, and disappeared. But I asked God what He wanted, and He'd made it clear through various signs that He wanted me to stay in the job and in the area.

And so I'm staying and am learning a good deal. Learning something about pride. About work-related things. Feel He is preparing me for something else. Some other work some day. Feel He wants me to stay because of what is happening in my family. Wants a chance to work in them— Pat, Katharine, Nate—in various ways. Wants us here at this church so that He can have a chance to work in us.

Jim also speaks about his job. Sketchily about jobs stretching back maybe 35 years. About how he's asked God's help and guidance along the way and how it had worked out. Worked out in unpredictable ways. Worked out well.

Elaine points out that any of these choices have seemed more like temporary things. Experiences that God wanted us to have before he asked us to move on. And I think of sets of rapids, boulders and ledges, separated by placid stretches of river and eddy pools. I think of the upper Hudson in particular. The parts above the Glen.

Curious that Jim and I both immediately began speaking about our jobs when trying to talk about God's control, God's guidance in our lives.

Sandra speaks about her relationship with God, about a five-year lapse in that relationship that she's just emerged from. About how God, if we let Him, will bring us to Him, but how if we choose to go our own way He won't stop us. And how looking back, she feels like, what was I doing? How could I live so empty a life? How could I let go of what I had?

The sense of a new blossom opening in her life, one of those huge roses big as dinner plates.

Jim speaks about the relief he feels that God is in control. That He has a plan for him. That it's a good plan. Can't understand how people can live without that sense in them. People who believe in no higher power. People who believe only in the operation of the physical universe. Nothing outside that. There's a brief look of perturbation—horror would be too strong a word—in Jim's eyes as he speaks, as he imagines such people, as he remembers maybe the days before he was saved.

Alpha Retreat. Weekend away from our everyday lives. Holy Spirit weekend. Jim arrives Saturday A.M. because of the tickets he's got to the basketball game Friday night. Elaine's sick and cannot come. Flu and cold.

Saturday morning in our small group, Jim tells the story of the visiting preacher at the Baptist Businessmen's Association meeting who tells him he will do great things for the Lord with young people. The story in which many young boys come to Christ after his talk to them. His voice thickens, and his eyes become red. Well up like two clear springs.

Saturday afternoon, Jim and I go canoeing down a creek nearby. His first time in a canoe. As he gets in and walks upright to the front, as the canoe wobbles back and forth, I'm amazed he doesn't go swimming. Put it down to how much of an athlete he is. As we make our way down and back up the little river, he strokes strongly. As though he'd been doing this for years. He appreciates the beauty of all the green and the birds and the big blue sky and the pellucid water floating us down over sand, but he's a city boy he says and that's where he likes it best. His son Cole likes the country, but Jim thinks him odd for this.

After our hour survey of current and leaf and bird and turtle and sand, we return to the put-in. Jim heads on up to play basketball with the two Toms. I turn back to paddling.

Skits Saturday night and Karaoke. Jim sings. We all sing, make ourselves silly singing silly songs. We have a glorious good time.

Sunday morning's clean-up and worship. Packing and leave-taking.

What I take away is a memory of deer browsing in woods near a field, an otter swimming up creek, the clarity of spring water flowing in the creek bed, being prayed over for the Holy Spirit, a brown hawk perching in a tree, fish rocketing over sand shallows, morning fog lifting off the creek, the loud sounds of a pileated woodpecker in the morning woods, the righteous feel of a paddle in my hands again, and a canoe flowing under Jim and me sure is as the perfect life.

# Kathy

Single. Fortyish. Looks thirtyish to these eyes. Works in one of those evangelistic para-church organizations. Pleasant. Sincere. Kind. Just so. Talking about moving out on her own after years with her roommate, Scotty. Time for her own place. Quiet. Joyful. Laughs a little like a child. Open like that. Delighted.

Home Fellowship. During sharing, speaks about a trip she took over the holidays to visit nephews and nieces. The cheap fare meant three hops. Two of them, she sat with a woman who was doing a dissertation for her second PhD. Was raised a Jew but practiced her Jewish beliefs only sporadically for decades.

Studying Christians in China, the history of Christians in China. Began with the study of Jews in China. Jews who had migrated into China along trade routes thousands of years ago.

Descendents could be traced by their names. She was apparently fluent in one of the dominant dialects and visited several times, spending altogether a number of years in the country. Asks Kathy, who makes clear she's a Christian, what she would say to an atheist. What she would say to a Muslim. (She had been married to an Algerian Muslim.) An agnostic.

Kathy responds as best she can, laying out the facts, her experiences, Scripture, the arguments. "I could see she was unsettled. She seemed hungry for the truth. She wanted more. The more I shared, the more interested she became. We exchanged contact information. Email. Phones. I felt God working there. Guiding what I said. Helping her to hear.

"Surely He's working in this woman's life."

Kathy. Spent seven years in Turkey. A Muslim nation of maybe 70 million people, 1000 Christians. Working there to bring forth Christ, to bring him before the Turks. Bring Him present to their minds. A people who, when they think about Christ and Christians at all, think about the Crusades. Think about modern Christians as descendents of the Crusaders. Murder and mayhem. Torture and theft. And loss heaped upon loss.

A geography where Saint Paul planted many churches. Where "Armenians"—the Christian minority in Turkey— were slaughtered by the hundreds of thousands early in the 20th century. Survivors fleeing into Europe and the United States.

Story. A Turkish woman, *au pair* in the States, returns to Turkey, where Kathy befriends her and leads her to Christ. Mother very upset. Her daughter has betrayed her family, her friends, her culture, her heritage. Some Muslims believe it's better to behead a family member in such circumstances because by doing so the convert's soul can be saved. Turns out, in this particular circumstance, the convert was allowed to keep her head. Couple years later, the mother is still outraged and again asks her daughter why she has converted. "It's the truth," she says, but then says it's not her job to convince her of the veracity of the Gospel. Shortly thereafter, Jesus appears to the girl's mother in a dream, who says to her, "You need to listen to your daughter about me." He then reiterates His words in John 14:6: "I am the way, the truth, and the life. No one comes to the Father except through me."

Another story. Two Iranian sisters. Came to the States to study and came to Christ in the process. Return to Iran in the 70s and eventually join Kathy's evangelistic organization. When they tell their father, he becomes very angry and won't talk with them. The girls pray for their parents to receive Christ also. Their mother comes down with cancer. Jesus appears to her in her home. He reiterates His words

141

in John 14:6: "I am the way, the truth, and the life. No one comes to the Father except through me."

Kathy's eyes flash sideways at me as she smiles. Within a month, the mother dies, she says. "Isn't it amazing? All the work He's doing?"

Kathy is full of stories and a wonderful storyteller. What makes her stories so engaging is God's presence in them and her excitement about His presence.

At one Home Fellowship, she tells a story about a trip she has taken to Thailand to attend a several-day meeting involving people in her company from all over the Far East. She notes that companies often have off-site meetings in Thailand so that their attendees may have access to the prostitutes, especially in Bangkok, a city thick with German and Australian men. Sexual tourists, they are called. A perk.

She prefaces her Thailand story with the comment that her greatest fear is that God will not meet her physical and emotional needs.

She is in a small bus, a *tuk-tuk*, in Bangkok, among the foreign predators and the mild Thais. Slowly the other passengers disembark, one by one. She has no idea where she is. She only knows the name of her hotel. She has no idea where it is in relation to anything else. She does know how to say, "How do you do?" and "Thank you" in

Thai, but that's about it. She can't even ask where the euphemism is.

The *tuk-tuk* driver has taken her to the nether regions of the city, out beyond where most of the people are, where there is little hope of finding anyone who has even heard of her hotel. She is the last one on the bus, except for a young woman. As the green lushness of the countryside reveals itself in front of her, a jungle wilderness, the young Thai woman asks her in perfectly good English whether she needs any help.

The Thai woman has studied English in school and knows enough to carry on a basic conversation. Once she understands what Kathy needs, she gives directions to the driver and stays with Kathy until they have located the hotel.

"I'm amazed at how God takes care of me," she says. "There I am, starting to panic. Having no idea how to find my way in this strange country. And there is God in this Thai woman, taking care of me. Letting me know He is there for me. Lifting me up. Supporting me."

As she tells the story, she looks side-long at me, eyes flashing, the lines at the corners of her eyes converging, opening, converging, opening, like a fan. Isn't this wild, her eyes seem to say. Isn't He extraordinary? I mean, don't you simply delight in what He does?

Lately, she's been speaking about buying her own place. Put a $61,000 offer in on a condo listed at $67,000. Even so, she will need more support. More underwriting. To make the payments.

Works in a worldwide evangelistic organization's HR department. Determines whether people are ready and have the right training for foreign assignments.

Asked whether her company has its share of self-willed people and politics, she says that she recently attended a meeting at which two different pieces of the organization in conflict met together to determine how to resolve their differences. She saw a real setting aside of personal and organizational agendas, she said. A real attempt to resolve the differences.

Brings a friend to the Home Fellowship. Work colleague. Back in the states after a year or so in Turkey. From Chicago originally. Nothing pious there. Honest. Midwestern straight-from-the-shoulder type of deal. Twenty-five maybe, but I don't ask, and I find my guessing to be less and less reliable. Thinking they're younger than they actually are, often by close to a decade these days.

Dreams the last couple of months that wake her in the middle of the night. Claustrophobic, sweaty dreams. Trapped feeling. Needs to open the window in the middle of the night and breathe deep breaths. Walks rapidly around, to feel the air passing over her body. Panicky. Fervid.

Barclay has her sit in a chair that Jim places in the center of the living room. Pulls a silver vial of anointing oil from his pocket. Prays over her, the whole gaggle of us, hands outstretched, some of the women touching, Barclay laying hands on head. Several of us speak prayers in addition to Barclay's. He features healing and casting out and blessing language. Others blessing and healing. Elaine reads scripture.

At the end, Barclay says he detects no possession or demonic influences. Kathy's friend thanks everyone, happy to be back among Christians again. She feels okay she says. No heavy feeling. Normal. Better.

After I'm in the Home Fellowship a year or so, she begins singing in the band. Regular there after Twila leaves. And she's strong backup to Pamela and sometimes Sandy. Apparently content to support rather than lead in this. But she does lead by being there in the band, one of maybe seven or so.

In Home Fellowship, she prays like this: "Lord, we ask that You just help Pat's foot to heal. You, Lord, are the Great Physician, and it is only through Your Grace that we can expect to heal. We know, Lord, through your Gospel that Your mercy is great and that You only wish good and beneficial things for Your children. So we ask that You restore

Pat's foot perfectly, that You heal it so that she can go on about her work and her care of her children, so that she can again walk and enjoy her walks through the neighborhood. Since Bill is here in Florida, Lord, she is alone and needs Your help. We ask this in Jesus' name."

Kathy's Birthday Party. We are three weeks into Alpha—a course of dinners and tapes and small groups on the basics of Christianity—and Kathy and I are helpers in a group that Jim and Elaine lead. We haven't met in the Home Fellowship in a month and a half because Jim and Elaine cannot do both. But it is Kathy's forty-second birthday, and Elaine has agreed to have the party at her house, since Kathy's and Scotty's apartment is so small. Kathy has invited Minnie and Billy and Scotty and me and Pat, my wife, and several people from her work and a batch of international students she's just met at a local university. There are two Filipinos, one Japanese, one Korean, one Hong Kongian, two Moroccans, an Indian, and one Texan. Billy's the Texan, and he's the weirdest one there.

The Japanese, Korean, and Hong Kongian are all young women, girls really. Late teens, early twenties. Hard to tell. They're giggly and travel from room to room, then outside, then again from room to room, together. They tell jokes about one another that make us all laugh.

Billy makes some of us North Americans giggle also with his talk of conceiving his son during a tango lesson in 1967,

146

or some such thing. And he talks of a weekend he spent recently in prison as the best weekend he's ever had. There were 36 inmates who took part, along with perhaps another 40 or 50 Christian men who weren't inmates, who were there to bring the story of Jesus to the prisoners. Thirty-three of the prisoners accepted Jesus as their personal savior. And now in the monthly follow-up sessions, it's clear to Billy that their lives have been changed and that the lives of their families are changing as a result.

We all swirl around Kathy, who seems happy and birthdayish, as she twirls around us. Effervescing. Inquiring. Laughing. Drawing us out. Caring for us. Opening her arms to us.

Everyone is wearing name tags, when I come in. Elaine's has her name in English, Japanese, Korean, and Chinese. Or names that are close to her name, according to her, according to the three giggly young women, she says. Where do I get my identity, I ask? Outside, she says. And so I go out and down the back steps to the patio made of red brick, and Kathy makes my nametag. My mark. My handle. My moniker. The sign I then set on my chest that connects me back millennia to people of whom I have no idea except that their names were William or Bill also, or something like that.

Where's Pat, everyone wants to know? She sends her apologies, I say, but she has to stay home to take care of

Katharine. (Pat and Katharine have moved now and have been with me for about three months.)

I meet Randy, who works in the same organization as Kathy. Divinity degree, but has never gone into the clergy. Struggled with it. With being on the outside of those politics, that center of church attention, that fulcrum of God's heavy lifting in the everyday lives and deaths of people. When Billy volunteers that I cook up powerful fancy good food for the Home Fellowship, Randy wants to know what I like to cook. Bouillabaisse, I say. What's that, he wants to know. I tell him a fish stew. Fish. Shellfish. It cooks a real long time, doesn't it, Billy wants to know. Well. Actually, I say. A pretty short time. I've often thought about opening a restaurant, I like cooking so much, I say. What kind of restaurant, Randy's wife Diane wants to know.

Well, an eclectic one, I guess. Eclectic? says Billy. What does that mean? From everywhere. No particular kind, I say. Well, I've thought of opening up one, says Randy, that has the Gulf of Mexico as its theme. Foods—especially sea food—and the preparations you find in the communities around the Gulf. Interesting. Very interesting. I say. Good idea. Lovely idea.

For awhile I watch Kathy as she speaks with others, serves the pound cake that Scotty has made and puts fruit over the top. There are two kinds, one with mace—a definite tang—and one without. We have our choice. I take either. Both. Delicious.

148

Kathy delights in things, thoroughly enjoys herself, tucks in her chin to smile and laugh. She squints and crinkles up her face around her eyes in an almost unwestern way, an oriental self-delighting, self-effacing way, a way that seems baldly profane and holy at once. Playfully profane, as if she were thinking, oh, isn't this naughty, and isn't this fun, when if there is any naughtiness, it is more made-up than real. The naughtiness consisting almost wholly in a play with naughtiness, the fun coming from a playing at something one does not quite do, at wearing someone else's clothes without permission, let's say, clothes that are either too small or too large or are the wrong sex and are therefore funny. As if she is watching herself try on these strange clothes and finds the whole thing absurdly silly and fun.

Loose in someone else's house with no one home trying on strange-fitting clothes, looking in the mirror and laughing.

But then there is also a certainty, a stillness, a gaze steady as the sun over water that lances through the laugher, the playfulness, that is quiet and inviting and reassuring and objective and imperturbable and implacable and outgoing and friendly and lasting and unworried and cupped and pouring, pouring, pouring out everywhere, pooling among us, rising warm among us, striking comfort deep into us. Striking freedom and a lightness deep into our chests and abdomens and limbs and heads so that one feels almost like one had been given a dose of a potent anti-gravity medicine and one were suspended just a fraction of an inch above, outside one's actual body, there in Elaine's dining room, eating pound cake and strawberries.

Then it's time for the cards and presents. We gather in the living room with its fireplace and old photographs and bass and couch and coffee table and coffee table books and comfortable chairs and big cabinet thing. Kathy sits on the couch and opens one after the other. Books. Scarf. Cards. Some other stuff I cannot see from way across the room.

I've given her Leo Tolstoy's *The Death of Ivan Illych* and Donald Hall's *Life Work*. Donald Hall was a professor at the University of Michigan a long time ago, and I took a course from him that changed my life. He's a poet who writes nonfiction as well. *Life Work* is a personal essay on the role of work in his life. Writing work. It's about how he works, when he works, what he thinks about work, what others think about work, what some others have written about work. Since we all work, it is a topic of some interest. His intelligence is lively and surprising and enjoyable. He is a generous writer and person. He keeps up a correspondence with thousands, I think. His knowledge on many topics is deep—literature of all kinds, Vita Blue, Ezra Pound, T.S. Eliot, baseball, Henry Moore, Robert Frost, hockey, the history and rhythms of New Hampshire rural life, *et cetera*—and his writing is first rate. The book alludes to his conversion to Christianity, which happened late in his life and which has apparently proved to be a difficulty to him in his relationships with his non-Christian, literary friends. His Christianity illuminates his work, and his work illuminates his Christianity. The book is quite an engaging good read. At least it is for me, someone who knew him a long time ago.

*The Death of Ivan Illych* is one of my favorite prose fiction works. It was written after Tolstoy became a Christian. Tolstoy introduces the reader to the Russian middle class, a group of people who are selfish and self-centered and unredeemed. Ivan, as ambitious and self-serving as anyone in his circle of friends, work colleagues, and family, has received an important promotion and is moving his family into a new home, more expensive than the last. In doing so, he injures himself, and the injury causes him to take to his bed in pain. The doctors can make nothing of it and can do nothing for him. Ivan's pain increases to extraordinary levels—to tortuous levels—as he comes to a number of important personal and spiritual discoveries, in isolation from his family, comforted only by his servants. It's a story of spiritual transformation through pain and suffering, of Ivan's coming closer and closer to God as he approaches death. Lovely. Powerful. Tolstoy gets at something fundamental about suffering and its divine potential.

Well, that's why I give them to her. Not sure that outside the Bible she's much of a reader, but there it is. That's what I've done. We'll see. One tends to believe what one finds pleasing, one's friends will find equally so. But my friends have often surprised me with what they like and don't like in books, what they've read and haven't, how much time they give to reading, how seriously they take it, what it means in their lives.

Back when the earth's crust was still cooling—in the early 1970s—one was considered profound in some circles when one said, "You are what you eat." For the new millennium, we should modify that old saw to say, "You are what you read." One truly does live inside one's mind and one's spirit, and these only receive a well-balanced diet when one is reading good stuff. Stuff that stimulates but does not titillate, stuff that instructs in useful things, that tells us about what works and doesn't among humans, stuff that brings us greater knowledge of the creation, of our fellow humans, and of God.

The thing about Christians, though, is that you can count on them to have selected—every single one of them—the same story to like, the one story that seems to explain things best. It's a story all of us have decided to live inside, surround ourselves with. To one degree or another, every one of us wants to talk directly with Jesus, walk with him, sit with him. Feed him, maybe. Touch Him. One can count on us to want to hear from or hear about John and Simon Peter and Paul and Mary and Martha and Lazarus and Timothy and Thomas and James and the rest.

One can count on us to want to enfold the outside world we live in with this story, with the people and the divinity of this story, and turn the brutal quotidian world into the glorious grace-filled place it was created to be. Count on us to want first-century-like Christians to appear like so many loaves and fishes and to keep appearing, springing out of the ground wherever we go. To want the world to turn into a gentle place for the first time since before memory.

Ten o'clock, I find myself saying thank-yous and goodbyes. Kathy stands in the entryway, and I'm awkward, having suddenly stumbled into my two-left-feet-hand-rammed-completely-in-mouth bashfulness mode, stammering to find words to wish her well. To wish her a continued happy birthday. To hope she will enjoy the books as much as I. To thank her for sharing her birthday with me. To say regrets for Pat and Katharine again. Well, I think. Be well, I say.

# Ken

Attends once on a trip down to see me with Grace, his daughter, and Nancy, my wife's sister. Call one another brothers-in-law, usually, to keep it simple. Friend for thirty years. Pastor of two Vineyard parishes in Michigan. John Wimber's startup that's now all over the place.

Yes man. Says yes to God. Yes to man. Honors. Affirms. Has been dropping little and big faith stones down my deep faith well for decades. My dry deep faith well. No sound. No sound. No sound is how it's been. Until a little more than a year ago when we both heard *kerploosh.* Both wet in the backsplash.

Their daughter, Maja, son-in-law Patrick, grandkids Isaiah and Wavy, make it down also. About the same time, but not exactly, and that's good because I don't have that much room. Patrick here on a conference, and they make a vacation of it.

Maja upset. Bouncing on her toes as we talk, and I disjointedly, distractedly prepare dinner. Boys like two marbles ricocheting around the apartment as Patrick tries to slow them down. "How could you? How could you become a Christian?" she accuses.

"You were my ally. You were my friend, Uncle Bill. You were my one support in my atheism with my family.

"What happened?"

"I read a book," I said.

"We used to have long philosophical discussions. And you told me to consider other ideas about how everything works. And I did.

"And now you're a Christian. Just like my parents. I can't believe it. What happened?"

"I read a book. It's reasonable. There's good evidence. Logic."

Silence.

"Usually there's an emotional part, isn't there? It's not just a rational thing. An intellectual thing."

"Well . . . ."

"Take my father."

"An extraordinary person."

"He worships his 'Heavenly Father,' but I've never heard him speak about his actual father. Not once in all these years. About those problems his father had. Or anything. Nothing. About his real father."

I frantically do this and that, trying to make the meal converge. Over-cook the steaks. Forget the napkins. Got them. Forget the water. Got that. Forget the salt and pepper. Flatware. Steak sauce. It's hard to hold up your end of a conversation about the meaning of life and death when you're trying to prepare dinner for five.

Isaiah wanting this and that. Excited. Weird being in this strange place with this strange man and the bare white walls of the apartment. The monk-like apartment. "Remote Uncle Bill. Do you have a remote for that TV?"

"Sure Isaiah. Here it is."

"Not now, Isaiah. We're not going to watch TV now."

"Bill," Patrick says, "we have a TV, but it's only hooked up to the VCR. He only watches movies we rent or buy."

157

"But you know, Maja, there are different sorts of causes of a thing. Saying that doesn't fully explain how your father came to his faith or how he sustains it."

Bouncing on her toes, "Are you correcting me?"

"I don't mean to. How can I? I mean."

Confused, I then say, "No. I'm not."

"But what are you saying?"

"Well, take a car wreck, for example."

"What?"

"Let's say it's been raining. Agent A is in a very big hurry. He's late for an appointment, and he's rushing to make up the time. (Or he could be a she, but let's say she's a he.) Because he's rushing, he's going too fast. He's distracted by a cell phone call. As he's speaking with the party he is late to meet, he slams into a truck that he doesn't see, that has just appeared suddenly in front of him, going slower than he's going.

"He skids into him on tires that don't have enough purchase on the pavement to stop him in time.

"Does the rain cause the accident? No it doesn't. It may provide an important precondition. But the cause is Agent A's great hurry and his distraction. He is inadequately cautious. He makes some unfortunate judgments, one of them involving the possible effects of the rain.

"If it wasn't raining, would he still slide into the truck? The answer is yes. Probably. But the damage would have been less."

"I'm having trouble following you."

"Your psychological explanation may tell us something about your father's initial willingness to believe. But it doesn't tell us why he continues to believe. I would contend there is a more complete explanation for this than you've given."

"I wasn't trying to be complete."

"I suppose it gets down to what sort of story you want to live inside. What story makes the most sense of things."

"There. That's just it. You've said it yourself. It's a story."

"It's a story. Yes. All explanations are stories."

"A story isn't right or wrong. Every story has its own validity."

"God manifests Himself everywhere, in many stories. Maybe all stories. Or all good ones. But some stories have greater explanatory power than others.

"And this particular one has the added benefit of being a history, not just a story somebody made up, a triumph of the imagination. It's history. A story that's verifiable in the events of the world. A triumph of fact."

"Well, that's another conversation. Anyway. Thanks Uncle Bill for this food. It looks delicious." She says this as she feeds Wavy and as Patrick feeds Isaiah. And I begin to feed myself.

"I think I may have over-cooked the steaks."

Then later, after the kids go to sleep, Maja, Patrick, and I stay up until about one o'clock in the morning talking about what we think about things, philosophical topics and everyday topics, just like three college students in a dorm. Except for the vacuum tracks in the rug. How clean the place is. As Patrick notes.

But back to Ken. Maja's dad. Whose biological father died the previous summer. Who has been attending a grieving group. Comes to visit my apartment and my Home Fellowship. Comes to meet the people I speak to him often about in our Monday night phone calls. To check up on me. Make sure I'm involved with some honest-to-God Christians rather than the indifferent kind.

Home Fellowship. Ken is here. Nancy's back at the apartment watching Grace. Someone comments on the loveliness of the words in one of the songs we sing. Ken mentions he helped create the words to that particular song.

Then he tells them about my doctorate in English, something I haven't discussed.

"Oh, so that helps me understand the words you wrote about our house blessing," Anne Marie says. "So you write? You still write?"

"Process descriptions. Business Plans. Reports."

"But anything else?"

"No. Not really."

"And it was in poetry," Ken says meaningfully.

"Poetry?" Anne Marie says.

"Poetry?" Susan says.

"What do you mean? He studied it?" Elaine says.

"No. He wrote it. Bill is a poet."

So that is that. Muse leaps out of bag, runs around the room, clawing its way up the walls until it rests, panting, inverted, claws embedded in the ceiling. "Well," a couple say. What I don't say is that I am not a poet. Haven't written a poem in years.

Later, back at my apartment, he says, "There's nothing mini about Minnie. Boy, is she something.

"Billy shows you can have Christians of all kinds. A real pistol of a Christian.

"Jim and Elaine. You'd think they'd be fully engaged with work and grandkids. But they've got the Home Fellowship and all their other church activities. Out there. Completely out there for God.

"You've really stumbled onto something, Bill. How'd you find them?"

"They found me, really."

"No pretense. None that I could see. No distraction into doctrinal alleyways. Just straight-ahead faith."

Monday's Ken's day off. I call him Monday nights. We kick around what we're reading, family news. Ideas that have grabbed us by the throat. We talk about God and quantum mechanics and cosmology and evolutionary biology (knowing only enough in some of these areas to be truly dangerous) and people in his church and the people in my church and fundamentalists and N.T.

Wright and Fredrick Buechner and C.S. Lewis and Brennan Manning and my son Nate and his daughter Maja and what we're thinking, like two college students talking about big life ideas together and where they go and how they proceed and how they get to wherever they want to go. And how we might follow them. What we might do. How we might bring their doing to pass.

Talk about things we have only read something here and there on, talk maybe that's only a little bit informed.

Talk about what Christ means and what God intends for Him to mean and what Paul has to say in the matter and who John might be and where he fits in. And why he is necessary. And we are talking literature now. We are always talking literature, whether it's the Bible or Lear or something else. About the human story told there. And in our hearts.

About the stories our hearts tell us back. About where they fit and how to fit them and where we sit or stand or how exactly we locomote through this whole disparate, modified, worried, sun-sprouted, paradox-enabled, blissful, turvy, tongue-laved, liquid, languid, hurried, blasted, bleating, ticking, wooly, wishful, turning, turbid, tingling, tickled, pellucid, pelagic, pregnant, preening, frazzled, frizzled, flaked, wilting, whimpering, simpering, splintering, erotic, eclectic, opening, lightening, broken, newborn, nubile, hectoring, hopeful, suffering, beautiful, charred, oozing, and cheery odd world.

One night, I ask him how he handles all the suffering and grief and sorrow he must see every day or nearly every day in his work as a pastor, and he says he cries. That crying helps a lot. That he has been crying more lately, and it seems to clean him, to purify him. To give him peace.

He talks about his dad and how difficult it has been dealing with him, dealing with his attempted suicide back when he was younger. And now especially since he's dead.

He talks about Maja and how the story of the prodigal son has seized his imagination and how he is trying to be as the father in that story. Trying to live with that spirit toward Maja. Maja who has had both her children with Patrick out of wedlock but who is now married for tax reasons, who seems to enjoy a certain anger toward her parents. An instrumental anger that moves from one to the other. And these days, Ken's the one feeling the heat.

Talks about the other kids, Nancy, church. But mostly talks about books and God and wants to know how I'm doing.

And after his visit, after the Home Fellowship and after he and Nancy and Grace attend church with me, he calls it all good. Pulls out the seal and stamps the whole thing good to go, the people, the pastor, the Home Fellowship. Says the pastor's southern rhetorical style is something he can't personally pull off, but that Mark seems to make it work quite well. Theology seems fine. A decided lack of pretense, of piety, of the non-essential thought baggage that some churches seem to accumulate and emphasize. Some Christian churches find comfort in defining the saved (themselves) narrowly, along the lines of whether one speaks in tongues or not or whether one confesses to a priest or not or whether one can be bitten by a poisonous snake and survive or not or whether one's church allows female clergy or not or whether one believes in creationism versus evolution or not. But my church, he thinks, appears not to want to do that sort of thing.

And after that, I feel better. Settled.

As I say, Ken's been working on me gently for about 30 years concerning my agnosticism. Gently. Not coercively. Giving me books. Asking me questions that are tough to answer. Showing me in his even-tempered, affable, happy, humble, gracious, self-deprecating, humorous, encouraging way what God can do with people who place themselves in His hands. He drew me toward himself and in so doing drew me toward God.

Plays disc golf, and is pretty good for an older guy. Beats me regularly. But he's a year or so younger than me; so it's understandable. Shoots a few hoops from time to time. Competitive. Follows the University of Michigan teams, sort of. Good writer. Has written a few books. Publishes his sermons on his church's web site. Five kids—one boy and four girls—ranging in age from about 30 to 7. Son—the oldest—works with him as a youth pastor, along with two other pastors and staff at the two churches.

Meat and potatoes man. Distrusts the exotic. For him, sushi isn't so much a food as an example of human folly. One might just as well jump the Grand Canyon on a motorcycle. Likes his tea loose. Tea water heated on the stove, rather than the microwave. A spot of cream. A porcelain cup. A right way, and a wrong way. A little fussiness there. Likes to wear cool sunglasses and drives fast. Drives a Chevrolet Prism. Low key. Tells funny stories about himself in sermons. Most memorable: the time he got lost in his bathroom.

Knows the Bible as well as his children's faces. Style is invitational. Relaxed. Forgiving. When we talk, it's a little like talking to an idealized version of oneself. After all this time, there are going-in assumptions about a similarity of thought and feeling, a mild surprise when there are misalignments, great interest to understand these with the thought that maybe one should change one's mind after all.

He's what I'd hope to be if I were a better person. Most untroubled man I've known. An excitement that one feels sometimes when one is in prayer or worship. An intimacy one is blessed to have been granted. A refreshment. A recreation. The right companion for a playful, kicked back, complete wander across the wide world, to

poke about its enormous three-D, no four-D, no n-D puzzle-
ment, its idea trove, its lush maculateness.

Hair thick and stiff as a lion's mane but short.
Glasses. Contacts. A student of harmony. Sings at Christmas with the relatives in the kitchen, at the sink, doing
the dishes. As a teenager, wanted to be a sports writer.
Bachelor in nursing—a fallback in case the Christianity
biz doesn't work out. Churches are growing at maybe
20% per year.

One Sunday, as we are leaving his church building in
Ann Arbor, an old civic theater his church has renovated,
he points out a family walking toward their car.

"A few weeks ago, their little boy died. Two years
old or so. The service was sad. Sometimes you get to
celebrate the life of the dead person. But sometimes it's
hard to come up with something helpful to say. Devas-
tating."

"The burial service?"

"Yes."

"The service?"

"No. The little boy's death."

"But shouldn't we feel happy when something like that happens. The boy has gone to live with God in eternity, after all."

"Well. But when someone dies, it's a sad thing also. Most marriages don't survive it."

(One of us should have reminded the other that when Lazarus died, Jesus cried. But neither did.)

"Survive a child's death?"

"A young child's."

"Even among Christians?"

"I don't know. I do know that man and woman there are having a very hard time."

"And what is the purpose of that?"

"What?"

"Suffering? Why does God allow it?"

"Freedom. Without freedom we cannot choose God or not choose God. The whole thing becomes a little silly." Like a train running around and around on its track, the little plastic men and women in the town static, going nowhere.

"But surely God could have found a way of allowing us freedom without the suffering."

"Hard to imagine."

"I think there's got to be a purpose to it, in and of itself."

"There've been lots of theories."

"Some think that it brings us closer to God. That He uses it to bring us closer to Him."

"Suffering is suffering. It's just there."

I was a little surprised by the lack of a theory, but I later supposed he'd read them all. Over and over. Heard them espoused over and over by the likes of me. And none of them seemed adequate to him. None of them seemed fitting. So he'd let the whole thing go, the whole topic. Just dropped it and moved on to things his mind could make headway on. Let God have it. Have the whole blessed thing.

Not long ago, we are speaking on the phone about Behe's *Darwin's Black Box*, a book Ken's recommended. A book that tries to discredit evolutionary theory on the basis that in specific organisms the combination of molecular-biological changes required to produce a new function (such as sight) would be highly improbable. The word "highly" here, if one is to believe Behe, is an enormous understatement.

I complain to Ken that the author seems to play both ends against the middle. On the one hand, as a Christian, he would apparently support the existence of miracles, highly improbable events. But he would not allow evolution because it is highly improbable.

One supposes that Behe would reason that he is merely using the rule of reasoning that materialistic atheists use to discount miracles and is applying it to one of their pet theories. Further one supposes that he is trying to show these non-believers that if one is not allowed to admit the materialistically improbable in one's explanation of things, one is simply left with a handful of dust. A mystery. Unless, of course, one allows oneself a supernatural explanation.

But I would argue that Behe gets himself or us or both tangled up in his tit-for-tat game and that he helps us overlook the possibility that the highly improbable and the miraculous are the same thing. That God works through natural means and that the highly improbable happens all the time in God's nature. That the possibility of the highly improbable is His way of entering in with real drama.

Statisticians know that statistical outliers happen all the time; every distribution describing large-number phenomena has data points at its extremes. Extreme extremes. Because such data points happen at a great distance from the mean doesn't suggest that such points are any less real or believable or admissible. They are just as real and valid and credible as any of the points associated with the mean, the median, or the mode. They happen, even though they do so at the end of the tails.

I suppose what really irritates me about the Behe book and others like it is that it plays to something divisive and ultimately destructive within us. Something that likes bashing better than it likes understanding. That likes polemics better than agreement.

Anyway, after I say something like this one Monday night on the phone, Ken (an apparent evolutionist, himself, in certain moods) remains reluctant. Unwilling to become as exercised as I am about what I accuse Behe of doing. Unwilling to become exercised at all. And I get tired. I wear us both out, I think, by how quiet he gets. So sitting there, breathing, not saying much of anything now, we move onto less acrobatic topics—family, the upcoming wedding of our father-in-law, discussions of the marrying and burying business (his vocation), status of my company's new mobile voice and data network. So forth, so on. The everyday stuff.

# Kim

ooks mid twenties, maybe. Says mid thirties. Blond. Single. Divorced a couple years ago. Travel consultant. Travel agent. Likes it sort of. A job like any other job, except for the perks. The adventures. Spring of 2000, Alaska. The last great frontier, she says. You must go there before you die. I can't tell you how beautiful. You must see it. You must be in it. Effusive. Determined. We must all go. Soon. The sooner, the better. Fall of 2000, goes on safari. Africa. Likes it. The difference. Maybe more like appreciates it. Is struck. Oh, the sun shines there sort of like it shines here. But the people. The people. So different in the way they live and work and think. But poor. Extraordinarily poor. Amazingly poor. Dirt poor. Living in the dirt. Living out on the land. Oh, yes. The animals are magnificent.

Her mother and father have struggled. Mother has wanted a divorce. Father doesn't. But they do it anyway. Father drinks. Years of angry back and forth. Drinks until he's drunk. Apologies. Again and again and again. The mother forgives and forgives. Now Kim's a little weepy.

But she smiles also. We lift her up. And her parents. Ask God to guide and comfort them.

At each Home Fellowship meeting, we fill out prayer cards. Each of us who wants prayer says so, and we each take notes on what each asks. Then we throw the cards into a pile at the end and pull one out, take it home, and use it. Sometimes, in the beginning, I don't speak up but write something for my family down anyway. Every few weeks, we pray for Kim and her parents.

One night, I make a dish from a recipe in my favorite cookbook. Wild rice with orange zest and pecans and olive oil and vinegar. Pork casserole with dried apricots and raisins, onions, and other stuff. Bib lettuce salad with orange slices. Fruity meal.

When I make it, grating the orange peel and sniffing the oranges, the spicy-sweet-piercing orange smell seems to me to have been fashioned in paradise. A smell that makes me think right away of God, something only He could do. Something of Him. I almost feel like He leans in toward me and breathes into me through those oranges.

That paradisal orange smell is still in my nostrils that night as I warm the casserole on Elaine's stove and as the wild rice mixture comes up to room temperature on the counter beside the stove.

Afterward, Kim comes over, admiring the food. Wanting the recipe. Tell her about the cookbook. She orders it. Has it now. Just got it. Hasn't opened it up. Can't wait, she says.

I used to drink. Sucked my soul right out of me. My hope.

I'd like to chat with her father sometime, if it works out. Maybe say something, a look. That will take. That will tilt him even slightly outward, away from what he knows too well.

Jim and Barclay suggest Al-Anon for the mother. Kim says she'll look into it. Meanwhile, her dad's moving out. Into a condo. Furnished. A blessing, really. All the way around. But it's a slow motion move.

Stops to speak with me in the church breezeway recently, smiling. Excited. "Bill, the pork's marinating right now in my refrigerator. I'm making your recipe! I can't wait. Is it better on the first day or the second, after you cook it? Did you do like they say and take the pork out and reduce the liquid down and then put it back in?"

"That's great! Well, I think it's better on both. Yes. Take it out first, and then reduce it. Definitely."

"I'm so excited to try it."

"Do you have a someone with whom you intend to share it?"

"No!"

"Well you'll enjoy it that much longer, then."

"Could be. We'll see whether I mess up or not!"

"I'm sure you'll do magnificently with it."

"Well, thank you. I hope so."

Sings occasionally with the band at church. Music team. Band. They used to be called the choir in the old days, when I was still uncrusty. My pre-voting, unwidened, extremist, fit, unlaunched, pissed, proud, hormonal, virginal, anti-everything, soon-to-be-post-Christian, pseudo, lachrymose, angled, talkative, quickened, hugely knowing days.

Now they've got a guitar, congas, rain sticks, tambourines, sticks and rattles of various kinds, organ, piano, keyboard, and recorded augmentation. Used to be the organ and a choir, but that's kind of boring now, what with all this other ornamentation.

Lovely voice. Nestled in there with the others' voices and the guitar, congas, rain sticks, keyboard, augmentation, and so forth. I like it when she sings. When she shares something about her day or her week. One feels livelier as a result, cared for, taken care of. One feels she has come out also, which one wants to help her do.

Alpha Retreat Weekend. Karaoke. Sings "Let's Get Physical," and as the words that she doesn't thoroughly remember appear in front of her, her face reddens. "Let's get animal," she sings. The red in her face deepening. Shaking her head like she's having a bad dream, maybe. The rest of us laughing at a Christian woman singing these things. And then she is laughing also. Her eyes reddening, welling up but not quite spilling as she blinks. Blinks quickly several times and laughs. And sings.

Home Fellowship. One gets the sense as she talks about her week that we aren't enough. That work and her church activities and Home Fellowship activities maybe need some augmentation. Some help. That there is too much of her to be expressed. Explored. Or her heart is too large. Our world too small. Or something. And that we—the current constellation of her life—should be expanded some way. Or changed.

Alpha Evening. Discussing her father, they just passed Thanksgiving weekend. Dinner at her mother's with her father. Watered down wine. Divorce is final now. Current big item in her father's life: prostate cancer. An operation to remove it planned. Turns out he's Christian. "But he doesn't believe like we believe, Bill. Doesn't have a relationship with Jesus. Like it's enough to go to church once in awhile. And that makes it bittersweet."

# Lucy and Robert

Not their real names. Robert. Barclay's long-time friend. Both long-time Christians. Friendly. Warm. Robert's got a general contracting business that he's just getting going.

Lucy develops curricula for an MBA program at a local university. Has a PhD. in business. Has worked all over. Sales mostly. The way she met Robert. They were both in sales at a company somewhere. She likes her current job because it allows her to write. Writing and business. What she likes best.

Robert prays in tongues. As we pray over Tori, who visits once—this night—and whose mother is very ill. Tori agrees to be a surrogate for her mother. Barclay leads us and applies the oil. We stand about her as she sits. Robert isn't obnoxious about it or anything. He says whatever he's

179

saying quietly, making room for others, but nevertheless going on in a manner that frankly seems odd.

Nate, my son, thinks it's all—tongues, that is—gibberish. When I was an agnostic, I thought so too. But now I've changed my mind. Maybe in some people it really is gibberish. Maybe in others it really is God.

If you read Paul, you get the idea that tongues is like any of God's gifts. Some get it. Maybe all get it, some to a greater and some to a lesser degree. If to a lesser degree, maybe it is somewhat gibberish.

Some say there was a time of miracles and there was Pentecost but that these are over now and we need to struggle through as best we can. I just don't think it can be that way.

Why wouldn't God want to be active in our lives? Jesus suggests that He is. That He will be. To expect that. The coming of the Holy Spirit. The flood of God into our lives. Paul suggests that He is. John.

If He wants us to pray in tongues—and Paul certainly suggests that this is the case—He will offer us this, and who are we to turn Him down? We are told that refusing God is a bad thing. Why on earth would we want to? Spite? Self-sufficiency? Pride? Tastefulness? Decorum? What are these in the presence of God? They seem mere bratishness under His gaze.

On the whole, I like it when Robert prays in tongues.
Odd. It takes me by surprise each time. Then I think, here
may be God, and I let its strangeness go. I glance at Robert,
his belly, his balding head, his trembling hand held out toward Tori, its palm toward her, as if to shine the power of
God on her from the delicate looking confluence of bone
and skin and blue veins that is his hand. I look back at Tori,
listening to his murmuring prayer as Barclay prays in English, then Elaine, then Lucy.

It is said that tongues expresses what one does not
know how to express in the language one knows. It is
said that it is a way the Holy Spirit signifies. In some
churches, worshippers aren't considered fully Christian
unless they pray in tongues. In others, it is vigorously
frowned upon. The topic's infected with the bacterium
of dogma.

So tongues is hard to speak about clearly (no pun
intended): Dogma mixes the opinion of men with the
Word of God. Whirls them together so that God's Word
is confused with our human ideas about how things should
be.

In the Home Fellowship, we seem to come from many
traditions, many styles of worship. In some traditions,
prayer in tongues is very strong. In others, almost non-
existent. So far, Robert is the only one in the group I've
heard pray in tongues, except perhaps for Minnie who

routinely utters a soft clicking sound. My hope is that he continues, if that is God's will.

As he prays, one is reminded that God is indeed mysterious, strange, and supernatural. That he can do whatever he wishes. That He is powerful enough to make normally sensible people do apparently extra-sensible things. That He can invade us, if we let Him. Take us over. Act through us as He chooses. Even if we don't let Him. God is God, after all.

One is reminded that He is here. And here. And again here. Present about our very beings, if we will only open our eyes to Him. Make a place for Him in the story of our lives, our everyday story.

God is like a Guest Who will only enter in if asked and if asked will patiently examine every corner of our lives, Who will take up permanent residence in our Guest room, Who will then outrageously insist on telling us what we will do and not do in our own homes, Who will insist on being attended at all hours of the day and night, Who will engage us in conversation at inconvenient times, Who will institute a new order, an Invader Who will gently but quite deliberately take over our lives.

Robert trembles as he prays, and this seems right. Straight-legged, back on his heels, subdued in tone, he prays saying what? Asking for God's mercy, perhaps, wondering about His will, saying he loves Him, that He is all-powerful, that He always knows best what is to be done, asking Him to comfort Tori and her father, to use this time of illness to bring Tori and her father closer to Him? Or perhaps he asks why Tori's mother needs to suffer, why suffering needs to exist at all, why at this time, O Lord.

Or maybe he asks or says none of these things. Maybe he says only sounds he cannot understand and in the saying of incomprehensible things, in the uttering of un-utterable ideas and requests, he stumbles toward God. Maybe he wanders in a desert at night with no moon to show him anything.

His eyes are closed. Perhaps in his prayer world there behind his eyelids, he enters directly into God's pres-ence, into His Being, the Unknowable, the Unknown Darkness deepened with billions of stars scattered down through time like glitter across His face, the Shepherd who in His perfect gentleness seems too exquisite to ap-proach, the Fire that burns white and blue and yellow and purple and orange and green and red, folding upon Itself, burning upon burning.

Or perhaps in his prolonged murmuring, he appears to disappear. One no longer hears him as one looks upon Tori and listens to the others pray their prayers. One listens and watches and discovers he has vanished as one thinks only of Tori and her mother and her need for her mother to be healed.

Another Home Fellowship. Lucy asks for prayer for the destroyed babies, the aborted fetuses. She prays outside an abortion clinic and asks us to pray for her as she faces those who don't want her there, and she asks us to pray that her prayers there are effective. That the women prayed over change, turn away from what they are about.

# Mary

Not her real name. Early thirties. She comes once.
Twila brings her. I remember sending her flowers the prior Christmas. Anonymous. Quiet.
Doesn't offer anything. Scared in the eyes, in the way
she manages her body and her things, closing these lat-
ter around her close. Others engage her over dinner.
Small talk. I hear them in the other room. Leaves early.
And as she's gathering, I'm afraid I haven't spoken one
single word.

# Minnie

illy. Her husband. His off-handed remarks. Spinning out whatever's whirling about his head, giving it whatever course it likes to take. Getting you off your point and onto his, with a big-toothed way that collapses his chin up under his nose in a yuck. Yuck. Yuck. Yuck. Faulknerian.

"Wull, there's no telling what he (presidential candidate Al Gore) would do. What that wooden excuse for a man would. . . . No. Wait. I'll say it differently. We all know exactly what he'd do if he got in there. Don't we now? He'd ruin everything. Every. Thing. He'd ruin everything. Don't you think? He'd destroy it just plain as. . . . Yes he would.

"I know you do." He is looking directly at me. Expecting an answer, maybe, as I shift my eyes back to Minnie, who meanwhile waits. Her head bowed over her Bible,

187

which looks like it has got itself wet once or twice in a good soaking rain. Thickened up like a cake.

She has been leading our Advent Bible study, freight-training through a long set of passages, having one or the other of us search them out and read them, then linking them back to one another. But now she sits off on a siding, awaiting her husband's pleasure—his coming and going—to wear itself out.

"Billy," someone says. "Let Minnie continue."

"Why I'm not. Why do you say that?" surprised look in his eyes. Mock hurt. A little amazed. Then smiles.

Minnie's closed eyes come open again, and she chugs resolutely on. "Bill, please read Luke one, thirty-nine to forty-five." I page back and forth. Back and forth.

I've seen Minnie made up to go out. Several of us go to a jazz club downtown one evening Billy isn't there. His sister has died after several years with Alzheimer's, and he is with his family, burying her. In Texas.

Minnie's elegant in her dark blue dress. Quiet. Sits at the other end of the table. Orders mussels, a bowl of them piled up, rounded up, shining black, same as Jim and me. The special. Only woman who does. Most of them, I think, afraid of getting their hands dirty. The messiness. Of getting the marinara sauce on their dresses.

Then too, the lowliness of the things themselves. Bottom dwellers. Or maybe they just don't like mussels.

The jazz is passable. Louder than needs be. Good trumpet. Bass. Handled some Miles Davis without too much specific nervousness. Loud though. All of it. A flawed competence bruiting itself.

But Minnie chuffs through this craggy, concussive topography as if it's nothing but smooth plains and gentle hills. Throttle set low. Careful. Deliberate on the up and down. Her husband's sister has died. She is going, but she is going slow.

I've seen Minnie made out all kinds of ways. Clown. Clown on Halloween. White with red polka dots. Blood speckling a white light. White face. Red globular nose. The Blue Serene at Milton's Jazz Club, feeding patiently on mussels: black shell, brown beast, red sauce. Sitting underneath the coruscating horn music, lifting even it up by her presence. The Church-Going Matron, in a brightly competent, serious but joyful dress. Sunday morning make-up. (Some but not too much.) Exhorting the congregation in the free prayer and praise time—the prophesy time—to hold up our shields of faith to quench Satan's burning arrows that would otherwise bring us unto pain and suffering and death.

Lady Guitarist in the evening, spinning out the floor of our singing. Our faltering and off-key, careful and loving, guttural and desultory throat noises that begin our Home

Fellowship. We are embarrassingly uncertain this close to one another and off, but her playing is always dulcet and delicate, a gentle tonal progress through words that are a comfort to say no matter the quality of the sound of our saying.

Then Teacher in her thin work dress, domestic get-the-housework-done dress, in the community center where the poor children come Saturdays to learn about Jesus, collect prizes at games, and take their snacks. King's Kids, she calls them. What she does, what we who help her do, what the kids themselves do, also. King's Kids. "*Shhhh*," we say, as the children's voices crescendo and then quiet again with our huge *shhhhhing*, admonishing, as one small girl's dress rises above her thighs to reveal surgery scars where skin has been puzzle-pieced together to heal what appear to have been iron-sized burns. Deep. Ragged. Angry pink and red. As a boy races for the bathroom, one girl takes a paper from another, and another boy picks up his sister and drops her back in her chair like a sack of onions. As another calls someone else a name and tells him, "Shut up! Miss Batter talking!" As Minnie rings the cow bell for quiet, for order, to make a brief space for God's mind to enter and find its place among us. Cow bell. New element. Ringing over ground that some decades ago entertained its share of chewing cows. Beeves. But now has gone to low income housing arranged in one story duplexes, asphalt, concrete, a few palms and scraggly hedges.

King's Kids. King's Kids day. Saturday afternoon in December. Sky blue as a bluet. Sun bright as a klieg light. A tall woman in tight top and mini skirt, an exposed throat and upper chest messily scarred, enters the room, asks me quietly for a pen to fill out a form. Fills it out in the back of the classroom. Hands it to me. Leaves. Returns. Asks a question. Leaves. Returns at the moment another surge rises in the sea of child noise. Shouts, "Sit down!" Angry voice, vicious. "Sit down and shut up." Looks at each of the twenty-some children with outrage in her eyes, possibly deadly rage. "I'm telling you sit down and shut up!" Silence or as close as it is possible for twenty-some children to get. "That's better. You keep quiet, now. Don't let me come back and hear that noise again. I will come back. Do you understand that?"

She scans the room again for a target. "Do you understand me? Miss Batter doesn't have to come here, you know. She doesn't have to put up with you bunch of screaming brats. You be quiet now. You listen to Miss Batter. To what she says." Slowly, rigidly she leaves. Tall in her high heels and thin body. In a rage she wears like a disfiguring scar, over a scar she wears like a medallion.

Minnie proceeds, quietly. The children are slow to recover, as if knocked suddenly to the floor. As if recollecting themselves after a sudden concussion. Recalling themselves from somewhere else. Finding it difficult to return.

As Minnie speaks, as she explains the drawing that has now been passed to each child and is duplicated on the easel she stands beside, a drawing of a warrior with a shield labeled "Faith," one of two band-aids on her right elbow loosens and, flapping, reveals a bright red sore. One of the children tells her to cover it up. Cover up the sore with the band aid. Her band aid is coming off.

She looks down at it, startled out of her fervency, surprised I think at her earthly body, that the body she has is wounded. And as she seems to recognize the elbow the child has pointed to, she smiles, briefly as if to say, "Oh, yes. There is that also." Then she folds the band-aid over and presses it down, but it doesn't stick. So she then pulls it off and rolls it in her fingers and sets it aside as she begins to talk about the breastplate of righteousness and the helmet of salvation and the sword of the Spirit, which is the Word of God.

The little boy I hold asks if he can color the drawing that he holds in his hands, his voice a whisper. He says he'd like to color it when he goes back home. "Sure," I say. "It's a picture made for coloring."

We, all of us, are made up some way, make ourselves up. Something. Make ourselves out to be some way or another. These are some of the ways I've seen Minnie be. Some of the faces I've seen her wear. Masks, of a sort, maybe. If they are masks, does it make sense to ask what the face looks like behind them? Is there anything behind these ways Minnie finds to be that one might glimpse? An essential Minnie? The Real Minnie?

One is often bothered by this sort of distinction, which rises up within one like a bad memory. The apparent versus the real. The essential versus the accidental. The fundamental as against the replaceable. Perhaps there is something to it—this way of thinking—when it comes to people, but one can make more of this sort of thing than it merits.

The other night, Minnie brings boxes and boxes of toys for King's Kids to our Home Fellowship. Donations from a few families in the church. Many that Minnie and Billy have purchased. Half used. Half new. Roll after roll of wrapping paper. Several tape dispensers. Half a dozen pairs of scissors. Labels. Ribbon. I carry some of it in from her car. Others get the rest.

Jim hurries us through the various stages in our meeting. Opening prayer. Singing. Bible study: Advent readings. Which Minnie leads. Special prayers for healing, discernment and guidance, travel. This particular evening, Barclay leads us in prayer over Elaine, who is the surrogate for Mary, object of our prayers for healing. Then it is Scotty's turn. Then Twila's.

Then it is on to the wrapping. Three set up shop in the Florida room, on the floor. Four of us set up on the dining room table. A couple others sit the session out, supervising. Observing. Watching the now weeks-prolonged election coverage. Minnie sits on the floor under the dining room table, unrolling and cutting and wrapping and taping.

The pizza arrives. We eat. Billy leaves. Barclay leaves. We resume our positions. Minnie, seventy-two, under the table, folded up almost as small as a child, carefully tearing and placing the sticky cellophane tape across seams in the folded paper until eleven or so. Until everything is wrapped. And then she loads her car back up. Trunk. Back seat. Front seat. She'll come back later in the week to pick up the guitar.

Next King's Kids is the party. Easel out front, when I arrive. Her old gray Accord. Martha's car. Brooke's car. Inside, Minnie in a blue jean jumper, and Martha and Brooke, the puppet show theater set up, one hundred and forty-nine gifts in boxes under and on three long folding tables, Minnie's face brownish from make-up, a rash there. A persistent rash. Long-sleeved white shirt to cover the sores and bruises. "Bill!" she says, right out loud, when she sees me come in. "Welcome!"

As the children and adults arrive and accumulate outside, Minnie circulates through the neighborhood, collecting more kids. About sixty altogether when she starts her program, some needing to sit on the floor. Five or six moving in and out at any point in time. I stand guard in the back, an eye on the gifts covered with old, freshly laundered sheets. Eye on the children, taking their warm, rough hands, hand on their warm shoulders, hurrying them back to their seats or out the door. Or in the door and in toward seats. Or toward the water fountain and back to their seats. Or into the bathroom and back to their seats.

One little girl, three or four maybe, eyes big as Christmas ornaments, angry as a terrorist. A scared little boy who hangs onto his older sister, who refuses to go in and sit down. A bad little five-year-old girl who won't go in and stays with me, holding my hand in the back, pulling my hand over her shoulder onto her chest.

Meanwhile, the teaching and singing and puppeting and clapping and child noise rolls forward inside for an hour and a half. Then it is time for gifts. Lines form. Gifts are selected and accepted. The community center empties out. Chairs put away. Floors swept. Tables folded up. Puppet show disassembled. Easel folded. Items placed in boxes. Boxes placed in cars. The old, gray Accord loaded up again. As the bright Florida sun shines down on the thin grass, the asphalt and concrete, the remaining children yelling at one another, the brick community center with a dedication plate bolted to it with the likeness of Dwight Eisenhower on it, Minnie sits in her car, sorts her keys for a moment, her forehead aimed at them, inserts a key in the ignition, and fires up her car, head wobbling a bit on the end of her neck, as I drive slowly away.

That is Saturday. The third Sunday of Advent, light make-up, matronly dress, after church, after she and Martha and Brooke have done the puppet show again for the church children, after she has served them all cake she has made, and aimed the knife with frosting on it into a plastic bag with a combination of hand and forehead, she packs up her gray car again with diverse bags and platters. Billy takes her guitar and the puppet canister into his car, thankful, he says, to have the use of his garage back, now that it has been depleted of gifts. As I leave, she is standing in the pine needles and grass underneath the wide, blue, egalitarian sky, chatting with someone beside her car. Someone. It could have been anyone. I forget now who.

That evening, at a party, black dress, gold in it, light make-up. Billy cruising our host's four month old house, checking it out. His desk—his old desk from his days at the diocese—is in this man's and woman's study, without legs, sitting on its drawers. Semi-circular desk, half a circle, half a world. Best office he ever had, built-in bookshelves he couldn't fill. It took the diocese historian to fill them.

At this party, Brian tells me his story over punch and peanuts. Two and a half years ago, he and his wife Debbie go to our church one day for the heck of it. Someone (Anne Marie) says try it. So they do. At random. Nothing in mind. Minnie rises and says there is a young woman there that day, unable to conceive. "God is a god of miracles," she says. "He wants you to open your heart to him." She does not know them. They do not know her or anyone at the church, except for Anne Marie, who is a casual and recent acquaintance. Just drop in. Then they leave. Shaking their heads.

Minnie's right. (They don't know to call her Minnie then.) They go grocery shopping after that, stopping in the isles, saying to one another, "What just happened? What was that? How could that woman have said those things?"

They buy Bibles soon after that. Begin to read. Come to church again. Again. Begin to meet others in the church. And then comes all the rest.

As he speaks, joy opening and illuminating his eyes, the muscles of his face leaping about under and around his teeth, his cheek bones, his jaw and temples, an artist animating himself, Minnie speaks in the kitchen quietly with someone else. Someone. It could be anyone. By the sink. Saying who knows what. The black dress draped over her, the gold shining down. And all around.

On another night, in the same season, at the Home Fellowship Christmas party at Jim and Elaine's, Billy arrives in a curly dark brown wig. "Makes me interesting to the young women," he says. Minnie laughs, shaking her head, laughs almost as though laughter itself were strange to her, as though she were still mastering this complicated skill.

Elaine's having us wear name tags because others are there. New church members. Friends from other places. Billy writes "Brett" on his name tag and places it directly over his sternum, a look of great seriousness on his face there, under the pile of brown hair, where a bald dome usually is.

"How do you like my new hair?" he asks me.

"It suits you," I reply. "Brett."

"Yes. Doesn't it?" he asks. "Haw, haw, haw!"

I catch Minnie at the buffet table. "I've heard Brian's part of the story about the day he and Debbie became Christians. I'd like to hear your part of it."

Minnie pauses. Tries to speak. Quiets. Sausage, bread, cheese, spinach dip, and shrimp on her plate. Eyes half closed in remembering, the eyes cloudy.

"We had just finished communion and were singing. I forget what. It was about two years ago. I had looked at Debbie during the service and had seen in her eyes her love of children. Her wanting one." She pauses. Tries to continue. Stops.

"The. The Lord urged me. We had almost come to the end of the service. If I didn't, the moment would be lost. I asked Mark if I could speak. I said there was a couple in the church that very much wanted a baby and had not been successful. She had been ill. But God had a plan for her. To have a baby.

"Debbie cried when I was done. I still pray for her almost every day. For her to have her baby. It has been a few years, but that isn't long for the Lord, you know. I'm convinced he will bring this about."

As she talks, I watch her. Small. Her forehead aimed at her plate. Eyes mostly closed. Cloudy. A small woman getting on in years. The two of us standing there in time, a particular party swirling around us. Particular people. Histories. Molecules. Atoms. Subatomic particles. Light. Shapes. Sounds. Space. A woman one knows, but only in a manner of speaking. She might as well be a character in a novel, a mid-ocean wave, or the aurora borealis.

"Isn't it amazing how He works in our lives, Bill? Did you know how Debbie came to be there? About Anne Marie?"

I say I do know about Anne Marie. Debbie had been in her restaurant with a mutual friend. Anne Marie had suggested trying out the church, in response to something Debbie had said. She'd tried the 8:30 A.M. service once but didn't like it. Anne Marie suggested the 10:30. Off-handed. Not thinking much about it. Thinking more about staffing for that evening than anything else. More contemporary. Not as stiff. Check it out.

After I speak with Minnie, Anne Marie tells me God has never asked her to do what He asked Minnie to do. "I wonder what that's like," she says, smiling. "I'll have to ask her."

Another Home Fellowship. A devotion provided by Scotty soaring across many passages of scripture and settling on forgiveness. A request for examples of forgiveness from our lives, the lack of it or the prevalence or the healingness or the how to. Minnie pipes in with those trumpet pipes of hers—soft-spoken, really, but one hears the quiet words as if God Himself were whispering because God is so much with her—and tells about her first husband, at Billy's urging.

About how after two children, he fell in love with another woman and left her, living with the other woman for a year until he finally divorced her. Divorced Minnie. And he didn't supply any money to help support the two children. But when college came around, he finally did supply the funds for that. And how God did lead her to forgive him, years later. But it was clearly a hard thing for her.

Then Minnie tells her own story of forgiveness. A story about her trip to visit her daughter's family with Billy. She made preparations concerning what she would do on the plane, what she would read. So she and Billy board the plane, and she is in the middle seat, while Billy is on the isle. A woman sits to Minnie's left, next to the window.

After Minnie finishes her reading and the plane is descending and the flight is concluding, she strikes up a conversation with the woman next to her and finds that someone in her family has recently died. That she is traveling to the funeral. And that Minnie has missed the opportunity to witness to her. To talk to her about God.

And the lesson she says she learned is that she is to not be selfish with her time in the future but to listen always to God and to what He has for her to do and to look for opportunities to do His will, even though it might interfere with her plans.

On the face of it, Minnie's story has nothing to do with forgiveness and everything to do with being faithful to God and His will, but I've learned that Minnie's wisdom is deep and that she is always on the point, whether this is apparent or not. And I conclude that what she's saying without saying it straight out is that God does forgive us when we fail to listen to Him and to do what he asks, if we are repentant, but that He does expect us to do better. And that just as He forgives us, so also should we forgive ourselves, after we have repented, and move on to the next opportunity to do as He asks and this time to listen and to act in accordance with what we hear from Him.

Hospital. Billy's about to have bypass surgery. Again. Another day or two. Sunday visit. He asks Minnie to pray prior to my departure.

"Lord, thank you for your many blessings, for Bill's visit, for your good care of Billy. Please continue to bless and guide Billy's doctors in all that they are doing and will do. We know that you have Paradise in store for each of us, and this lightens all our hearts. The prospect of joining you someday in Heaven. Meanwhile, please protect and keep Bill and his family as they travel over the Thanksgiving holiday. We ask these things in Jesus' name. Amen."

# Pat

Wife. Life partner. Lover. Child-rearing colleague. One with whom tenderness is the least uncommon. The person who has the most to forgive me for. Who knows the full range of my shortcomings, sins, character flaws, *et cetera,* best.

Generous. Enormously generous, until the generosity is not reciprocated.

Has dived into the sea of her children when they were born and only periodically surfaces for air.

More energy than three or four usual women.

As forgiving as Christ had in mind for us to be.

New to the Home Fellowship. Comes a couple of times before we break for Alpha. Tries it out. No pressure. No Christian. Maybe someday, but certainly not yet.

Enjoys it. Wants to learn more about this Christ from these people. Trusts them.

Would you like to come to Alpha, I ask. No, Bill. No. I don't believe in it. But then a few weeks later, as Alpha approaches, she says, well maybe I'll come.

First Alpha small group session, when asked what she hopes to get out of Alpha, says, "My son became a Christian a few years ago and now wants to be a minister. My husband has become a Christian. I've never had any need for it. I grew up in a family that used religion to cause pain to one another, the Catholics versus the Protestants. My father's family against my mother. As a nursing student, I watched people die who shouldn't have. So I haven't seen the point of it. But now that my son and husband have become Christians; I want to understand it."

She seems to enjoy church. The singing. The people. Deeply impressed with Minnie and Elaine. The others too.

Of course, Elaine and I talk. Minnie and I. Jim. Susan. Kim. Kathy. The others now and then. Others in the church. About how Pat is doing. How she's coming along. What she thinks of the church. Of Alpha. Of this Christianity thing. They ask. I believe some of them pray.

I say she's doing fine. God's at work there. He's doing what He intends to do.

Ken asks also. "Well, there's that Rozell (Pat's maiden name) control thing. It'll take some doing. I don't get the sense He's having an easy time, but He's holding His own."

"But you know, if she's able to relinquish to anyone, it would be God," Ken says. "Don't you think?"

"Right. That seems right."

At Alpha on Halloween night, Pat and Jim and I are talking. Jim wants to know where I've gotten the cupcake that I'm busily ramming down my throat. "Minnie," I say.

"Minnie?"

"She just had her alternative Halloween Jesus party. King's Kids."

"Oh, that's right; it's tonight. Or was, I guess. How'd it go?"

"It went well. Lots of kids. Lots of noise. Lot's of fun."

"Didn't we do that last year?"

"Yes. You and me and Minnie and Diana. We were outnumbered ten to one."

"At least that."

"Twenty to one, maybe."

"When Bill first told me about Minnie and the Halloween Party and the poor kids, I couldn't believe he was doing that," Pat said, looking way up there at Jim. Then she looks at me. "I didn't say anything then. But I couldn't believe it."

But then she misses most of Alpha to be with Katharine, who has play practice, homework, etc. To shuttle her. Help her.

"What'll Pat do when Nate and Katharine are gone?" Elaine wants to know.

"Not sure," I say. "But God knows."

# Scotty

On the early side of her forties. Perky. Single. Sorting out what to do, where to land, now that Kathy is moving. Works in the same organization. Administrative support.

Energetic. Sympathetic. Lively. Hopeful.

How do their minds work, these women? Why are there so many of them here?

It is said this Home Fellowship is a kind of family for them, the unmarried women. Susan has said it. Anne Marie. Elaine.

But it's a kind of family for all of us, isn't it? Perhaps it's just a statistical anomaly. Or maybe it's easier for single women to give themselves over to a group like us than it is single men. Or maybe life itself is harder for single women alone. Or easier for single men alone. Or maybe men whether single or married have difficulty getting themselves into these strange intimate affiliations.

Family a man can understand. Sports affiliations and card playing affiliations and drinking affiliations men understand. But a bunch of friends sitting around talking about God and one's feelings and one's problems and one's hopes and one's fears and one's frustrations and one's relationships and one's work and one's relationship with God. Talking about what God says to do and not to do and what one does and does not do in response and what one should do and not do and when and how to make Him happy. And still more, talking about what love is and isn't and what our ailments are and who is dying and who is trying to commit suicide and how much pain and the funerals, to include ovarian cysts and uterine growths and acid reflux and glaucoma and pre-cancers and cancers and bypass surgery and arterial repair and damaged discs and so forth. A bunch of people thrown together because they choose to be, mostly from the same church.

All of it just plain strange from a man's point of view. Or certainly from a recently agnostic man's point of view. Or the point of view of a man who nevertheless is not into sports or drinking or card playing or hobnobbing with other men, except at work. A man who outside of family is a solitary fellow. A fifth wheel. A loose cannon. A lost penny. An out-riding data point. Similar maybe to many other men.

And maybe this is really it, how men—many of us— really are uncomfortable outside of work and family. How we have no idea how this sort of thing is supposed to work or really what it does at the level of living, at the level of understanding that only comes from living a certain way. Our living doesn't inform us about this. This intimacy with nearly perfect strangers. This intimacy one doesn't ever achieve with one's actual family.

One has only hearsay to go on. What one reads in books. What others say. The point is, anything could happen, according to one's actual experience. Because one's actual experience is vacuous. One's imagination gets perfect freedom then. And of course that's kind of scary. Like a random universe is scary. Like an infinite number of monkeys at computer keyboards is scary. What will they come up with? They could literally write down anything.

But night after night at the Home Fellowship, one gradually stops thinking about monkeys. One does begin to understand that these people won't actually bite or make funny noises or swing delightedly from the rafters. They won't snag rattlesnakes from a cool place under the back porch for unspeakable rituals. They won't hold one down by force and do vague, unimaginable things, their faces contorted with a wicked pleasure.

One is actually allowed to maintain one's own person, control over one's own person. One is merely offered friendship and fellowship and various examples and views of what the Christian life is about. Rather bland, actually. Wonder bread and sliced cucumber and mayonnaise, salted and peppered to taste. The least remarkable of meals that turns out, oddly, to be quite filling and refreshing both. A blessing in its modesty. Its lack of spiciness and novelty. Its outward lack of ambition.

The fear that one inevitably arrives with melts away like the snow pack in spring high country, trickling and then rushing and then roaring toward the season's end.

During the time I've attended Jim and Elaine's Home Fellowship, I've seen Scotty's fear melt. Partially. As mine has. Hers has been profound and life-long, beginning with abandonment and other abuse she suffered as a child. Mine has a less clear source but arguably has run just as deep for different reasons, recalling different early conditions.

Thirties. Even late twenties. In most of us, the self hardens around like ice that won't be broken, building thickness and heaviness. Others distract us. Our work. Our adult toys. Our adult pass-times make us forget ourselves awhile.

But it's always this heaviness, this unyieldingness that we come back to. These thoughts that spew from our minds like a fountain in deep winter. Ice tower. Ice mound. The memory we have of all we have done and not done. Only love heals this. Only love washes this pure heaviness and coldness away.

Women seem to understand this better than men. Earlier than most men. I don't know why. These women here, in this Fellowship, have come to that, I think. Why they've come so early in their lives into this odd affinity. This arbitrary friendship. This deliberate love.

The usual relationships. Family. Old school friends. Work friends. Even church friends, in most cases. Don't work for what one needs, finally. Or don't work particularly well. For a particular sort of thing one might be said to need.

What one seeks is others who also have failed to wash away the excrescence that has built up on their surfaces. The cold, hard crystal of the self's history. The heaviness of one's choices. Others who seek help in washing this away. Who are determined that they will together, however briefly, apply love's spring until the mound of their everyday has been diminished. Oh, this isn't absolute and forever, certainly. Not at all a quick fix deal. Effects are gradual, cumulative. Deconstructing and constructing go on alternatively, periodically. Seasons in contest. That sort of thing.

As I say, neglected. One day, Scotty stood in the street. Toddler. She is told later in life. A neighbor's German Shepherd grabbed her by the back of her training pants and lifted her up, trotted her to safety on the lawn. Adults all around. In and out. Everywhere. But only the dog has the sense to drag her away from the traffic. That's why she thinks she likes dogs now. Big dogs especially, she says, as she pets Anne Marie's big white dog Hunter, a German Shepherd.

Little girl look to her sometimes. Open, fixed look to the eyes.

Lately she's been standing up in church, during the time allotted to God to speak back to us. The whole service devoted to our singing and speaking to Him. This small but very elastic portion of the program that we give over to Him to say to us what He wishes.

Not a time for people to say what's on their minds. A time for people to share with us what God's got on His mind. A bit of Scripture, usually. Sometimes an idea, figured or storied in some way. An admonition. Rarely a prediction but sometimes that. Generic, garden variety prophesy. Old Testament kind of thing. Makes one think twice or maybe three times about getting up. Speaking. Not many do. Something daunting there about offering up God's words, about getting them right. Even hearing them at all is a problem for some of us.

Hearing His word for ourselves is hard enough. But then hearing His word for others. That just sounds very difficult. And then what about when He makes it only kind of clear what He wants you to say or if He wants you to say it. Or I should say, what if you only kind of hear what He wants you to say or if He wants you to say it.

One week His topic for Scotty is Jeremiah 29:11, which she reads and then speaks about. The plans that God has for each of us. Not our plans. His plans. The trick for us being to listen carefully enough to Him to understand what they are and act in concert with them. Bring them into being. Idea is that He hasn't forgotten us. That He cares for each of us and wishes and plans good things.

Concept is that we have faith that God's will for us is beneficial, that He will provide what we need, even if we cannot see this now. That we have no business worrying about this, about how He will take care of us. That we merely need to have faith in Him and discern his will. Work in concert with His will, not against it.

She speaks of times in her own life when she has had no money and no way to pay her bills, and yet God is able to take care of her. This is speaking directly to several members of the congregation because they speak back as she speaks and thank her and God. "Yes!" "Thank you, Jesus." "Oh yes." "Lord, thank you." "Alleluia." "Almighty God." Their expostulations sounding almost as if they are interruptions. Preemptions. But they aren't. It's just that their enthusiasm and their affirmation have been surprised out of them, suddenly released.

Later, after the service, as many of us are standing in the breezeway and the sun is pouring down like a cosmic ladleful of unwoven yellow silk, I thank her for sharing the Scripture and her teaching with us. "Oh, thank you for the encouragement," she responds, quick as a reflex. "I don't know what it is. God just keeps telling me what to say, and I wonder, Do you really mean that God? And He keeps telling me He does and He wants me to speak His word. But I think why me Lord? And He says, 'Why not Scotty?'"

"Sounds like you should probably do what He says."

"Ah, yeah. I don't think He's giving me much wiggle room there. Course, if He did, I wouldn't be getting up. If I thought it was maybe just me, forget it."

We let the breeze blow through and the sun tangle down. Looking at one another. Smiling at one another. "I can't believe what you're doing," she says.

"What?"

"The sacrifice you are making. For your son."

"Well."

"How long has it been?"

"I moved here March 20th last year." It's April. Late April. The Sunday after Easter.

"I wonder if your son realizes the sacrifice you are making for him. That must be so hard. It really must be."

"Oh, you know. He's pretty busy."

"All that love, and I bet there's not all that much coming back right now."

"Well," I offer, again. Not knowing quite what to say. I mean, we love one another, my son and I. But a seventeen-year-old boy in his senior year has a lot of things on his mind. Then throw in that we are moving his home out from under him and relocating it 1200 miles away. And on top of that, I've been living away from him for the last year, which must feel something like abandonment or betrayal. Not that he'd put it that way to anybody, including himself. It would seem absurd, after all. But turns out our emotions are about as rational as Woody Woodpecker's. His and mine and everybody else's.

"Well. He's seventeen," I say. "He's just got a lot going on right now. Besides, I was an ungrateful snot when I was his age. He's doing a lot better."

Anyway. Scotty is one of those people who makes you feel better than you did before you started talking to her.

She's busy all the time that way. Like a summer lake I once canoed regularly. Cazenovia Lake. Cazenovia, New York.

During the month of August, Caz is quite beautiful. Reflecting, mostly. Four or five miles long. Quarter mile or so wide. Deep blue on August days, weedy from all the nutrients the farmers around there pump into the soil. Weedy even the day after the harvesting machine putts around yanking weeds from the lake. Enough weeds to fertilize the county.

A lake busy with weeds and sky and sun and waves in an afternoon breeze, all of it swelling underneath my canoe like an architecture of grace. An architecture of peace. Sustaining my boat and me stroke after stroke, glide after long glide. A generous, cool uplift in contrast with the air's heat.

Water that could have been anyone or any living thing, could have come from anywhere. Could have cycled through anything. Water that might have inhabited Socrates' eye or Abraham's finger or Hedy Lamarr's cheek, that might have coursed through a dinosaur or a vole or wooly mammoth, that might have arrived on this planet on a meteor or been born here out of condensing gas. Might have sustained Columbus on the Ocean Sea or wetted Jesus as John doused him in the Jordan or turned a turbine and lighted a light bulb for Elvis Presley in a Las Vegas hotel room or whitened the peaks of fifty thousand foot mountains millions of years ago or quenched the thirst of a coal miner deep underground in 1924 or poured over Niagara Falls or sustained a rainbow after a violent, killing storm or swelled a leaf in the Tree of Heaven that ornamented the lawn of a friend of mine or flowed down the Ganges carrying fecal matter and many dead or crystallized on the skin of an early, high-altitude aircraft in the nineteen fifties or sliced through Yosemite Valley in a glacier tens of thousands of years ago.

Water. For washing literally and otherwise. Dousing. Birthing. Baptizing. Shaving. Showering. Putting out fires. Drinking—an internal washing. Takes care of dirt. Sweat. Sin. Liquid fundament. Oceanic purifier. The blue in the blue planet we only metonymically call the earth. Life's first place, one speculates. First necessity.

Earth's blood, coursing through rock. Channeling. Capillary. Internal rivering. Pumping up, down, sideways. Surface rivers and lakes and oceans—the way the earth sweats in its spinning work. Rain the way it drinks.

Curving on its surface in a glass or a valley or hole or in the great wide spaces between the continents. Imitates the curve of all space.

And under me, Caz lifting me up on its tangled surface. Its weedy hair reaching up to brush the canoe bottom. The canoe I call my rocket; it is that quick. A one-man racing canoe. Cool and blue the way it pushes us up toward the sky, and the sky is in it. Reverent clouds.

Like that. Scotty makes you feel as if you were gliding along, easy like that, a long expanse out there for gliding.

Another Home Fellowship. Scotty's leading us in a devotion. Selected Scripture readings. Teaching and reflecting. Finally ending with forgiveness as the topic. Forgiveness. God's fountain in a parched world.

Several of us discuss times when we have forgiven. Times when we forgive. Scotty discusses her childhood. The neglect. The physical abuse. Repeated. Over a long period. And how she has forgiven that.

Someone says forgiveness is giving up the role of judge. Giving that to God.

And Minnie discusses her first husband. His leaving her when she had two small children and little else. For another woman. No financial support from him. Divorced. Abandoned. And how she has come to forgive him that.

And Scotty never knew this, how Minnie has been hurt like that. Even Minnie has been mistreated terribly. And then Scotty bursts into tears and refuges in the kitchen, with Elaine following. The sobbing reverberant there.

Until later when she is able to return and discuss it, how now she is starting to imagine maybe someday seeing a man, thinking maybe she might be able to love a man after all. But that's so frightening. It's so risky. A man could do anything, after all. He could leave her. He could abuse her. This after decades of decision, of a refusal to consider this sort of thing at all. A man at all. Forever. And now that refusal melting like ice in spring, disappearing, trickling away. And this absence of resolve, a familiar friend, this dwindling away is itself frightening.

A new place with new rules she never thought she'd get to. How can one possibly live in such a place? It's maybe a little like the picture C. S. Lewis gives us of heaven, where the grass wounds one's feet at first, where the light stabs one's eyes, where the bushes brushing against one's flesh are like rasps dragged across it.

And by the time I leave that night, we are talking about how Elaine has said something someone has taken offense to. Someone in the Home Fellowship. And how she has written and apologized and asked to be forgiven. How she does not mean anything by it. She did not realize. She was just being funny. Just cutting up.

And Scotty says we should be able to relax in the Home Fellowship and maybe not be as careful as we need to be elsewhere. How this is our Home Fellowship after all. How this is a kind of family that accepts us and loves us and can be counted on to take care of us. How of course we do not mean one another harm here. And I say that is true. And that is certainly how one should think of it. And that Elaine should not feel so badly.

Because Elaine is now saying that she will have to carefully watch what she says in the future so that this sort of thing doesn't ever happen again. How she just won't talk much. And we say—Susan and Scotty and I—say no, Elaine. That won't do. You don't understand. You have apologized. Now it is up to the person to forgive.

And later I learn that Scotty spends the night because she stays so late that it would be a major effort to get back to her apartment. And that Elaine is happy she decides to stay. And Jim.

Church a few months later. Scotty's been away at training, out west. Standing there singing. (By the way, it is a joy to sing praises to the Lord, isn't it? Times, there's a tingle in the spine, flutter in the diaphragm. Been that way since I was small, singing "The Doxology." Singing "A Mighty Fortress is Our God." Singing "And Did Those Feet in Ancient Time." I'm reminded of C.S. Lewis's "Transposition." The Holy Ghost playing the strings of one's being like Eric Clapton plays a guitar. Easily. Authoritatively. Masterfully.) Suddenly she's there beside me on my right. Black dress. New glasses. Lost a little more weight. Wonderful there. Right there. Close. Joy in her eyes.

On my left are Pat and Katharine. A little over a month since they moved down. And I want to introduce everyone because somehow Scotty hasn't ever met them, but we are worshipping, and introductions will need to wait for later. But it's confusing there with Scotty on my right, my wife and daughter on my left, and the not knowing, the one and the others. A year of my knowing standing to my right not knowing the lifetime of my knowing standing to my left, and the lifetime of my knowing ignorant of who I'd in part become there on the other side. Confusing how to worship together with all these disparate unknowings.

When we get to The Peace, and we pass it to one another, embracing all around, I make the introductions, very pleased now, less confused, and Scotty says as we transition into the next part of the service that it's amazing how much love there is here. And I agree and agree as her eyes shine like windows looking out onto God's Glory itself.

And then a Sunday a few weeks later I ask Kathy what's happened to Scotty, who hasn't been to church in awhile. And she says the Lord has led her to another church. She really didn't want to leave, she says, and there was nothing that happened, nothing negative. Just that the Lord has asked her to go to another church. She prayed about it for weeks, but there it was, and a denomination Scotty had said she'd never visited. But there it was. God's will for her, and of course she would obey.

Kathy's Birthday Party. "You abandoned us," I say. "You aren't coming to church anymore. What happened?"

"Well Bill, the Lord wants me to go to another church. I'm not sure why. I'm just letting Him decide this. I'm not going to push anything. I'm turning it completely over to Him. I'll do what He wants me to do and to see where that will lead."

# Susan

Short, blond hair. Late thirtyish. Parents intellectuals. Professor father. Professor mother. Single. Writer. Editor. Children's school books. Web-based children's instructional materials.

Lovely voice. Sings in an amateur group. Soprano. In church, when she sings next to one, it is a great gift.

My first night at the Home Fellowship, Barclay prays over her for healing, for the evil to leave her. To come out. Blessing her with oil applied to her forehead. We all pray that she will be well as she cries in gratefulness. Amazed that she has asked for prayer for a case of the sniffles and gets prayer for her very being and an exorcism to boot.

Some of us place hands on her lightly. Others not at all, a hand held out, palm toward her as though directing the laser light of one's soul into her. It is Barclay who holds on hard to head and shoulder and neck to make the healing hold. To let the evil in her know he means business. Won't take no for an answer. "Come out," he says. "Come out," in a sudden loud voice, sudden soft voice. Intolerant voice. As she sits there stiffly, crying for the affliction to please just leave. Leave her alone. Grateful, as I say, for the help.

Weird night. Odd night. Reminds me of the days when I was a boy watching Oral Roberts on the TV striking lame people on the forehead with the palm of his hand.

"Heal this man," he would say, yelling, the word "heal" landing itself like a blow.

"Jesus, heal this man," he would yell, his face contorted, his black long hair shaken loose from the shellac job it had started out in. "Jesus," he would say, as though the suddenness of the word and the loudness of it would maybe coerce the healing somehow into happening.

"Jesus, heal this man!"

And the man's head would snap back so hard I thought his neck might break. And the man would seem to stagger in his canes or his wheel chair. Seem to back up a step. Then Mr. Roberts would grab hold of the man's head and would seem to squeeze it like a grapefruit. And then after a moment the man would lunge out and walk on his own.

He'd walk down the long ramp under his own power, attendants in white coats following along with his chair or his canes. Apparently, a well man now. Healed.

I don't even now know what to make of Oral Roberts. But I'm sure God does do extraordinary things. All the time. Jesus leads us to expect this. It's up to us to open our eyes to see them. Healings? Certainly.

Recently, Ken, my brother-in-law, has been reading books about cosmology and quantum mechanics and evolutionary biology. I've been reading some of the same books. Had been, rather. Now it's mostly Christian literature.

He's blown away, as anyone should be. Telling me recently about the experiment with light and two slits, about the particle theory and the wave theory. About one explanation for how the light is able to do what it does in this experiment: photons and electrons take an infinite number of paths. Think of that! An infinite number of paths.

Was also telling me about chaos theory and probability theory and how events unfold in a probabilistic rather than a deterministic way. About how if you wound the string of time back up and let it unravel again, it would undoubtedly unwind a somewhat different way. Of what the implications of this would seem to be for the classical philosophic problem of free will versus determinism. About how somebody should go have a little chat with the Calvinists, the folks in the predestination camp. About how somebody should show them the math.

A couple of weeks before this, he was telling me about how gravity is a declivity or warp in the space-time continuum. About how light is the one constant in the universe. (I was reluctant to tell him how that is now in question with some recent experiments done by some British researchers.) About how atomic clocks have been placed on airplanes and flown around and how their time has turned out to be slower than that of atomic clocks here on earth, because of their travel. About how light may in some sense be timeless. About how God and light are one: The intuition of the ancients.

And now he has discovered string theory as well, something I haven't read about. About how subatomic particles may very well be one dimensional strings vibrating in unique ways. That matter is based on these strings vibrating as stringed instruments vibrate. About how matter itself may be making a kind of music. How matter itself may not be matter at all.

The great thing about Ken—one of the great things, I should say—is his capacity for wonder. And in all these conversations we've been having about his readings in quantum mechanics and cosmology, he has just been blasted away by the extraordinary-ordinary-miraculous-ridiculous-nonsensical-recalcitrant-paradoxical-sublimely-puzzling-ultimately-beautiful structures lying at the heart of the sensible universe. As he and I and all the rest of us should be.

He's brought this stuff up with engineers and people with science backgrounds in his church, and many of them seem to have no idea. No real understanding of all this sort of thing. As though it were enough to plow through life, occupied with one's own rather narrow concerns. Not looking up to try to peer at the world around and get at it, penetrate through to what makes it work. To these quasi-mystical ways that matter and energy and gravity—the quasi-physical universe—really behave.

Oh, neither one of us is a scientist or mathematician. We don't pretend to really know this stuff in the way someone in these fields would know it. But as one reads those who should know, the translators, one comes to feel that one does in fact have a grasp on a bit of this weirdness.

But back to Susan. Was she healed? Did Barclay and the rest of us make a difference? Did God intervene?

She appeared to be healed and vitalized. Natural or supernatural, that would be God.

One day, Epiphany Sunday, back in Florida after a week with my family up north, we are leaving the sanctuary after a particularly moving service, when Susan says to me, "Happy New Year!" Joy strobes through me like sunlight through the lens of an eye.

One night. Early spring. Home Fellowship. Studying Brennan Manning's *Signature of Jesus*, she says she likes the previous chapter better. The one on the dark night of the soul. On God's remorseless love. On the absence of God in one's life. His apparent disappearance.

The instant chapter—the one following—which is about God's out-and-out love, His kindly love, she can't relate to, she says. She hasn't experienced any of that lately.

Chat following dinner about why we both like the previous chapter, why it speaks to us more directly. Then we are interrupted. Diverge. Then she finds me puttering with the songbooks and picks the conversation back up. And as we stand there by ourselves in Elaine's living room, Susan's eyes fill. Empty. Fill. Empty.

Maybe it has to do with a man she's loved. Who could not handle her emotions. Since then, she has not been as intimate with God, she says.

"Maybe it would be different if I had a family, the intimacy of that. So much of my life is meaningless.

Work. I know that's true of most everybody. But that doesn't help."

"Maybe you want a change," I said. "Maybe God is helping you to change. Remember Galatians. Chapter five, I think."

I open Galatians and read her a couple of verses.

"We are made for joy, you know. We are made to love. When we don't or can't, we aren't right."

"But there's this time problem. I've wanted to do a Big Sister sort of thing, but I don't know where to find the time."

"Well. I know. It sometimes isn't clear how to work it out. But maybe God can help. Maybe He would know better."

Well, one never knows whether one says helpful things or not. One listens. One tries one's best to hear and to say what one is told to say. To listen when one is told to listen.

It seems a lonely thing sometimes. Just living.

We are all at odds with ourselves and one another. If we align some way, it doesn't seem for long. Unless we are with God. Unless we walk with Him. And even then, we seem to slip away in spite of what we think we're doing and find our own path—separate from His—and get ourselves into a wallow.

Nirvana. The limitless high plateau. Doesn't seem to be in the plan.

"Being a Christian isn't easy," Susan says, as her eyes empty again, and she uses one of my tissues.

"Maybe it's a human thing," I replied. "We just have all this pain and other junk inside us. Stuff we think is terrible. And then we think we ourselves are terrible."

"Like me here tonight," she said. "In the morning, I'll feel awful about all this."

"Well, right," I said. "But you needn't. We all have this unpleasant stuff in us, and we are here to help one another with it. And of course discover what God wants. Just so you know, I've got the same junk in me. A cosmos of it."

And again as we speak I am pierced by joy as I looked into Susan's eyes and see love and the need for love and pain and the need for relief from that pain. Joy as sharp as a needle to the heart.

"Have you read any C. S. Lewis?" I ask.

"Yes."

"He's kind of less interested . . . . He kind of pushes us not to take our emotions too seriously. Emotions come and go. Idea is to look past them straight at God."

"Yes. *Mere Christianity.* I've got some of the others. Haven't read him for awhile."

"Well. Emotions. Sometimes they get between us and God. Take us off in another direction."

I finish putting the songbooks away. Anne Marie comes in, sits on the couch.

"He brings us back, though, also," she says. "Sometimes he uses our emotions to bring us back closer."

"You know. I couldn't have had this conversation with Minnie," Susan said, looking at me with light and dark working in her eyes.

"Why's that?"

"She would have stopped me early on by saying something like, 'You aren't deep enough in His Word.' Or something like that."

"My mother won't have certain kinds of conversations either," Anne Marie said. "She contracted polio when she was five and was sent off hundreds of miles for a year to a hospital. Her parents visited her once a month. Can you imagine?

"So when I was a teenager and wanted to talk with my mother about normal teenage angst, she wasn't interested. I was hurt, confused. Didn't know why she was so unfeeling. 'So?' she said. 'So what? Is your homework done?'

"It was only later when I learned about that little five year old being sent away and shut off from everyone she loved that I understood."

"It's getting late," Susan says. "I need to get going."

"Me too," I say.

Jim and Elaine have spent the evening at the opera. Minnie and Billy are helping Mary Maud up north. Barclay has left early. We are largely on our own. Have the run of Jim and Elaine's.

Susan leaves. It's almost twelve o'clock. Anne Marie and Scotty and Twila and Kathy and I lock up the place and go our different ways.

Theater festival in town. Ten days. Troupes in from around town, around the country, the UK, Canada. Second weekend. Last couple of days. The Home Fellowship crew taking in a number of the shows, fanned out all over town. And I'm determined to see some of it. One act plays. Poetry readings. Singing. Dancing. I come out of Movin' Maury's one man show in which Movin' has been singing R&B hits from the fifties and sixties, tap dancing, stripping, telling life stories about divorce and performing and ministering and now love, how love is the main thing. How everybody should love everybody. How he's putting a place together in Texas for old people and children, because they're good for one another. Because both of them need more love.

Billy and Minnie are supposed to have joined me at this show, but I'm glad they haven't. Because of the stripping. I wonder where they've got to as I exit, and there's Susan, waiting for the three of us but gets only me. We rush off to find a show we might like, across downtown, walking fast. We can't find it, passing worriedly back and forth in front of the place without knowing it, like penitents in front of eternity. We find it in time, but the show's sold out.

Across downtown again, we stand in line and are lucky, we think, to get 2 of the last 3 tickets. We go in. Get good seats in the front. Two odd English women in baggy men's clothes and men's hats and moustaches direct the seating. Then they transform themselves into two odd English women in satin (or nylon, I can't tell) house coats who crack jokes, the one quite overtly come-hither and narcissistic and the other quite the character actor, the Stan Laurel and Granny Clampett of the two.

Various skits in which they play "Women From Around the World," which are stereotypes and parodies of stereotypes and parodies of parodies of stereotypes and parodies of parodies of parodies of stereotypes, ideas one can easily sweep up from television's bits and pieces. "Women From Tubeland" is what they might better be called.

Talking vaginas, pantomimes of various sexual acts, cavorting about in black underwear, and a final exposure of breasts is what we get. As the antics and laughter unroll, I can only wonder why we are all doing this. A packed theater. Eighty to a hundred of us jammed in there. Lucky to get tickets, we're thinking, some of us.

One point, the character actor backs up to a wall, her arms levered back up over her head backwards. Looks like they'll pop out of their sockets. Contortionist. Looks painful. We of course feel ourselves to be cruel for mildly looking on. She seems cruel for subjecting us to this. I close my eyes. She picks me out and announces to the audience that I am so overcome I am closing my eyes. She offers to allow me to help. I stumble out of my seat. She says just pull the arm down. It's dislocated can't you see? No problem. Just pull it down. I stand there looking up at her on the stool against the wall, and I can't do what she's asking. It might really hurt her. So I refuse and sit down. She got herself into it. I expect she can get herself out.

Another guy volunteers. He's a doctor on television, he says, so he knows what he's doing. A doctor, she asks.

A real doctor. No, a television doctor, he says. Oh, she says. A television doctor. He gets her out of her predicament with no more fuss than a stone dropping through deep water. Long pony tail, which the woman fondles sarcastically, as if it were a fake relic. Actors playing actor for us with one another.

After it's over, Susan says it was funny. Interesting is what I say. Yes, it was funny also. We both agree it was funny. Funny in a funny kind of way. Uncomfortable sort of way.

I walk her to her car over by the Methodist church. She blasts off. I blast off. It's late, and it's been a full day.

Months later at Anne Marie's restaurant, we gather for Susan's birthday dinner. It's Twila, Elaine, Jim, Anne Marie, Alice, Ed, Barclay, and a friend of Susan's from work and his friend. Scotty is ill. Minnie and Billy are taking care of a grandson. Kathy has a meeting. Carol doesn't have a lot of extra money or time to spend on these entertainments.

August is the traditional break month for the Home Fellowship. The group breaks off its study and goes out, plays games. Has a good time.

The birthday girl's forty this Friday. She gets cards all round. Three books from me. Fredrick Buechner's *Telling Truth: Gospel as Tragedy, Comedy, and Fairy Tale*. Seamus

Heaney's *Door into the Dark*. And Graham Greene's *Travel's with My Aunt*. (These are in addition to a book I've furnished her recently, Anne Lamott's *Traveling Mercies*, which she likes immensely.) A bottle of wine and forty one-dollar bills from Jim and Elaine. Etched wine glasses from Anne Marie and Michael. Several other things from the others that I don't actually catch.

I'm between Twila and Elaine, two pretty good talkers, who talk a lot about Mary and Jeanne. Mary's the physically abused child of evangelists who Barclay lifted up to the group almost a year ago. Can't work because of all the physical problems. Many, many major operations. In her early thirties now.

Jeanne's the woman Twila befriended and counseled who the Home Fellowship found destitute and high in a downtown park during August two years ago. Crack addict for awhile. Living on the streets. Daughter somewhere.

Well, yes they both pick up Mary and drive her to her doctor appointments. And they are glad to do it, but she is interested in making a day of it each time, arranging her appointments so that lunch is an integral part of it, and long conversations ranging over many topics can be traversed, and the problem is that they have their own lives and they need to get on with them also. And it happens that Mary saps one's strength and resolve and joy, somehow, just drains one, with discussion after discussion about her physical problems, her seventeen major operations and what the next one will be and who will perform it and whether he is the right one and just exactly what the objectives and procedures should be and when it really should be and whether she is ready for it and who will take her and who will come visit her afterward and who will take her home and what the probabilities of success will be or should be or could be given any number of assumptions and circumstances and contingencies.

One is simply depressed sometimes listening to the long string of problems and difficulties and conflicts with others and disappointments in others and discussions of her poverty and how she can't possibly make ends meet and where the money will come from to do this or that and how the closeness and smallness of her life seems to close in upon them and squeeze them until they are quite out of breath and gasping and nearly expired by the time she lets them go. And how sometimes they will simply call her a cab and pay for it rather than endure all this and spend the time they don't really have anyway because of all their commitments to family or work or their other ministries or all of the above and how they feel guilty about not giving her everything she seems to need but maybe she needs way more than they can give anyway. And oh, they hope I don't think they are terrible for saying such things, and they worry that maybe they are, but it just seems sometimes like she is too much, too much, or maybe it is something in them, that maybe they are less than they should be.

And through all this Susan's been talking with folks to her right and her left, smiling, laughing, enjoying her wine and her food. Submerged in the conversations, in the tastes of the wine and the food, and the tone and color of the ideas. In the wellwishing and the encouragement. In the concern and the laughter. In the funny stories and the interesting stories and the sad stories from each of us telling each other what we make of what we've come across, been given, had taken away. What we find ourselves doing, what others have done, what events have unfolded and how one after the surprising other they roll and jounce and spin on 'round a corner or a bend or over a rise.

Certainly Susan is back in God's arms, has found Him again and is resting in Him. She's smiling again and laughing. She's easy again. She has told me the week before or maybe two weeks it is that she's seeing a counselor who is Christian and who uses prayer as an integral part of the counseling process. How this counselor has a theory that when one experiences loss, the inevitable result is anger and grief, and if these emotions are put off, are put out of one's mind, they will inevitably come out. And how after her former boyfriend had bid her adios, she had buried herself in busyness and had refused to be hurt in any significant way and now years later has suddenly plunged into the anger and grief she had put off at the time, more than five years ago now.

But this is the big Four-O. The big turning point. The pivot that takes a young man or woman definitely into middle age. And here she is pivoting just fine, joyfully sipping her wine and talking. Talking. Talking and laughing. All through the appetizers and the meal and the dessert. All through the gifts and the stories. All through the well wishing and the cards with funny punchlines and funny pictures. From the prayer at the beginning through the leavings one by one as we leave, wishing her well, wishing her an excellent evening and thereafter.

Sunday. After church. After Pat and Katharine have moved down, and we have a house now. After Alpha has started, and the Home Fellowship at Jim and Elaine's has been suspended for Alpha, so that Jim and Elaine and Kathy and I can help with Alpha. After Minnie and Billy have been hosting what is left of the Home Fellowship in their home for a month and a half—Ed, Susan, Robert, Lucy, Anne Marie, and Kim meeting there. We stop and talk in the breezeway. Pat and Katharine have left early so that Katharine can get to school to apply make-up to the actors in a school play that is to be put on that day.

"Speaking about work, we were just speaking about it in the men's group I attend just before church, and it seems to me there isn't much guidance in the New Testament about how one should behave. A normal person. A person at work. How one is to apply this Christianity to one's everyday work life. How that works.

"I mean there are plenty of illustrations of how the disciples—more or less full time ministers—should and shouldn't behave. But one isn't exactly sure how to translate that into one's actual life. A life that is made up so hugely of work. Seventy or eighty percent of one's waking hours and a good part of one's dream time too."

"I know. I sometimes feel like oh, what are they thinking? The decisions management makes sometimes. One feels uncomfortable with them. Compromises. Customers' timetables. What has to be done, one is told, but has it, really?"

"Jesus didn't die with money in the bank. He died a criminal. As the world measures people, he wasn't a success. And yet here we are, trying to be successful in the way the world measures success. Financially successful. Professionally successful."

"Right. And you know, people at work get so exercised about things. Really upset and wound up and almost desperate sometimes, when deadlines are approaching. Or whatever."

"Yes. It's kind of like, look. Don't you understand we live in an eternal frame. An infinite frame? Don't you understand that this week or this year isn't the right perspective? Oh, we'll work it. We'll get it done by the deadline. Fine. But let's get a little perspective here. I feel. I almost feel."

I pause as Tom comes up and chats. After he leaves, Susan says, "You were about to say something."

"Yes. I feel a book coming on. There are just so many issues here. And few people seem to be wrestling with them. At least in books. They're certainly wrestling with them in real life. It's like we've got two worlds. The world of faith and the world of work. And there isn't much communication between them."

"Yes. I agree. You play this role at work, and it's so seldom you break out of that."

"Yes. There's this sense that there is the real me and then there are all these roles that I play. But one wonders whether if one is not the roles that one plays, what the real me might be. The roles one chooses ought to have something to do with who one is, shouldn't they?"

"They should. But sometimes they do seem to disconnect. The role and the person. And at work, trying to find someone you can get past the pleasantries with, who you can talk about something serious with, as we're doing here, is just very hard. I do have someone who is older than me and reluctantly takes direction from me who sometimes. Who sometimes I can actually talk with about something. And of course that's what the Home Fellowship is too. A place where we can talk about the things that matter without these roles getting in the way."

"Well. There's certainly the getting-in-the-way part. But there's also the expression part too."

"Right. I do feel good about what I do sometimes, about helping children learn things they should know. And that is there, underlying the other."

"Yes. But I guess where I start out on all this is whether any of it is legitimate or whether we're all off in the wrong direction. Whether we all oughtn't to give up everything and become missionaries or something.

"Well, I've got to go to work. Someone's waiting for me to help him count." I moved down the breezeway toward the office.

"Count what?"

"Money," I replied, shrugging my shoulders. Smiling.

"See you next week."

"You have a good week," I say.

Monday night. A bar downtown. Closed except for this theater festival benefit we attend at Jim's invitation. From the Home Fellowship, Jim and Susan and me and eventually Elaine. Twila and Travis are supposed to come but don't. Kim and Barclay have said maybe, but they don't show either.

Theater people—actors, directors, producers, writers, patrons, etc,—mill about, at first formally but soon loudly and informally as the number increase and the alcohol drifts down throats and up into heads, and the ceiling shifts lower, and the walls inch in, further and further. Smoke thickens and hangs. The glasses fill and empty. Fill and empty cheerily. People bend eagerly over the tables where the silent auction items are. Bend and write their bids. Bend and write their bids. Free wine until it runs out. Free food until it runs out.

Susan and I chat about various things. Her colleague whose mother died this fall, who lost a baby she was carrying last summer, and whose husband was just killed in a hunting accident last weekend. Katharine, my daughter, and how good-looking she is and how ambivalent I am about her theatrical ambitions. Susan's father and his building of a cabinet for her bathroom. Susan's renewed interest in dating. My Thanksgiving weekend testimony at Ken's Vineyard Church in Ann Arbor. How well Alpha has gone.

Jim joins us on and off. Chats on and off. Shakes hands with the men. Hugs the women. I ask him how he got involved, and he says that the festival board members saw him so often at the festival plays, year after year, that they figured they could persuade him to help.

Elaine finally shows. Says she was putting together invitations to another party. Couldn't break away. Had to get it done. Also lost her purse.

Jim mentions Barclay's been calling Elaine. Sounds lonely.

Susan volunteers to call Barclay and invite him to her work party. A general discussion of the appropriateness of this. Just a friend, she says. Besides, it isn't good to be alone during the holidays.

Elaine knows a fifty-year-old man. Good-looking. Divorced twenty years ago. Would Susan be interested? Sure. But fifty is the upper limit.

Then as the four of us talk, it turns out that Ed is separated from his wife, which explains why he sometimes hangs around town on the weekend rather than go back home.

Then I count up all the people in the Home Fellowship or who have visited the Home Fellowship in my time here that I know who have separated or divorced. Seven. Signs that there might be two or three more. Out of twenty or so. One-third to one-half.

And then it occurs to me that to God, we must seem at least a little like the Corinthians or a bunch of high school students. Coming together. Breaking up. Coming together.

Breaking up. In one several decades-long high school dance. It must drive Him nuts.

It gets late. A theatrical event is running along in the corner. A pantomime with dialog. A maestro-looking white-faced fellow. Black outfit. Clownish (red noses, frizzy hair, makeup) woman and man. Man tries to please the woman with gifts, which she quickly tires of, revealing her evil nature, as the maestro has predicted. Becoming more and more demanding. Less and less sweetness and light. Susan and I leave. We hug. We devolve to our various cars. Drive home.

# Tori

Thirties or so. Actress. Model. Comes one night only. Mother's ill. Comes for prayer and fellowship. Barclay with his oil and the rest of us pray over her. Robert in tongues. May seem weird to her. One cannot tell. Would to me. First night, and to have oil and hands laid on and tongues over one. What else will these people do, one might ask? What won't they do, if they insist on these oddities. But smooth as glass about the whole thing. Talkative. Positive. Open as a Bible on a minister's desk.

One sees her at church, but she hurries in and out. Sits way over on the left, at the row-end, near the wall. Little chance for talk. Must like it like that.

Months later, after months of prayer. Many emails back and forth between Elaine and Tori that Elaine forwards to the rest of us. Her mother dies. After a long struggle. Passes over.

Absence for a time at church, then she attends again.

# Twila

Not her real name. Reticence alternating with good humor inhabits a body that is fully-womanly, fully-fleshed. A Monroe ampleness. Slightly cross-eyed looking. Never sure which one it is and sometimes whether either. Finally one learns about the glass eye. The live one replaced when she was a child to eliminate a cancer. Thirty-five maybe. Couple of kids. Boy and girl. Husband. Comes to the Home Fellowship without him, the family agnostic.

Dazzle-Dent smile for the Home Fellowship crew. At church, she sings beautifully into a mike, chorally. So as to disappear in the sound of the choir and the band. The worship team. To uplift it but always to understand it. A stand of thin pines behind her moving slightly in a breeze. Then it's all business herding the kids on out through the breezeway, into the parking lot, and back out into the wide world. Typically, Travis (not his real name) stays home. Once in a while we see him there, which all of us remark on. He attends general parties, etc. So we've come to know him. New Zealander. Friendly. Likes to laugh. Easy going. We do pray the Lord will draw him.

Out there. On her own in some important respects. Fully capable, one believes. Firmly grasping her life and taking it forward. Leading her children.

Tells a story about coming to God. Conversation with a clergyman about her new interest in God, about her desire to have her new baby baptized as well. Occasion for laughter and jokes now.

How she explained her situation to him. Living with a man for many years. Father of her new baby. They'd never thought up a good reason to get married. But now the Lord was speaking to her, about herself and her new baby.

"Living in sin," he says. "Living in sin."

Well, work with me here, she says, or something like it. I'm trying to sort these things out. I think the Lord is talking to me. Maybe whispering might be a better term. I can barely hear Him, but this is what I think I'm hearing. Him. Do you think I am? I mean, what should this be like? Am I hallucinating or something? What is He like, anyway? I think He's wanting this baby to be baptized. I think that's one of the things He's saying. Does He say things like that?

You need to baptize your new baby. How important is infant baptism to God? Would He push me in this area? Or are you supposed to wait until you're older, anyway. I've heard that, but He seems to want this done. Can you baptize my little boy? Would that be okay? When can we schedule that? I think He wants it done pretty soon.

"You're living in sin. I can't baptize your baby as long as you're living in sin."

I imagine him with a surprised, self-contained look on his face. His eyebrows raised. The folds in his forehead arched. Mouth pursed. A just-so expression in it. Comedic. Dead-pan.

I imagine her looking at him, eyes wide open, her glad ten megawatt smile fading from her face. Like she wants to but doesn't get the joke.

"As long as you choose to live in sin, you will not be welcome in this church. There will certainly be no baptism. Good luck to you."

Not God bless or anything like that. Hugs her. Cordial expression now. Twila, in the blue funk women sometimes go into following birth, postpartum depression. He hugs her. She can't quite believe he does that. Gesture of affection after all that uncaring, that intolerance. That hostility. Still just looking at him, with her mouth open a little. Stunned. Deer in the headlights. Eyes wide.

"Thank you for stopping by. Lovely chatting."

Or something like that. Anyway, now she laughs about it. Him.

The spring a year before I arrive, she and the rest of the Home Fellowship move themselves to a local park for the evening. Bible study in the park, under the trees, sky, beside a carp-thick lake. Woman approaches them. Rumpled. Dirty. Depressed. Disoriented. Vague from too much alcohol and from living in the park for three days. Asks for help. And they do.

Money. Mammon. And moral support. Jeanne, not her real name. Starts going to church again.

Twila befriends her. Friend. Someone to talk with. Ask advice from. So forth.

Jeanne cleans up her act. Gets a place to live. A job. Kicks the booze. Makes a place for her daughter again. Who has been in and out of jail. Most recently, she's out.

Ends up clean. Three years later, still clean. Living now in another state. Thanks Twila and Jesus for how everything has changed.

Home Fellowship. During sharing—praise reports— she speaks about her son in elementary school. "Why are you so mopey?" she asks, as she is tucking him in one night.

"Nothing."

"Certainly there's something."

Silence.

"What is it?"

Silence.

"You seem kind of sad. What's going on in there?"

"Dad has a lot of worries. And sometimes I'm not sure God exists."

"Seems like a lot to think about."

"It is."

"Well, how about if you ask Jesus what to do," her eyes playful. Smiling.

"How do I do that?"

"You can just ask Him."

"I don't think praying will work."

"Well, let's try this. Lie down. Yes, right here. Put your head on the pillow. That's right. Now close your eyes. Very good. Now since Jesus likes celebrating with people, eating and drinking with them, that sort of thing, maybe you would want to picture him at a table with good things to eat and drink."

That sounds like a good idea to her son. He tells her that he pictures a table full of the kind of food that he likes. Hamburgers. Hot dogs. Candy. Coke. Then he pictures Jesus there, dressed in the sort of robes people put on him in books.

"Okay. Now, what's your first question?"

"How do I help Dad?"

"Okay. Go ahead and ask Him."

The boy closes his eyes and lies very still for about five minutes, saying nothing. Then he opens his eyes. Calm. Peaceful.

"What did he say?"

"He said to tell him I love him and do things for him. Help him if he asks for help."

"Well, good. Did he say anything else?"

"Yes. He said Dad's problems are his problems, not mine. That Jesus had given these problems to Dad for a reason and that together they would work them out."

"Well, what do you think?"

"I think Jesus knows what He's talking about."

"So, what else? What else do you have to ask him?"

"I want to know how He exists. God's supposed to be good, and all things he does are supposed to be good, but there is a lot of suffering. And suffering doesn't seem to be good."

"Why don't you ask him about that too?"

The boy lies back down and closes his eyes. It's about ten minutes this time. When he sits back up, he says, "*Hmmmm.*"

"What did he say?"

"He said, 'I *am* good. But of course you already knew that.'"

"What else?"

"He said that I should come to Him whenever I have questions or concerns."

"Do you think you will?"

"Yes. I think so. I liked talking with Him."

"Why?"

"I don't know. I just did."

Another Home Fellowship. During praise, she tells of her experience the Friday night before when members of our church and members of another church worship together. As she is singing and listening to the visiting choir members sing, and as she looks at several of the individuals from the visiting church, she hears "fake" in her mind. Fake. And there is something evil in it, maybe, she thinks at the time. She doesn't know what to make of it, but it bothers her all weekend. It keeps recurring. She keeps hearing it.

Like it is something God wants her to know, finally. But she doesn't know what to think, whether this is God telling her or her telling her. Whether these people are somehow fake or real or some mixture. They have come to worship. So why would they be fake? What are they doing there if they are fake? Are they evil? Or just superficial? Or misguided? It doesn't make sense, but there it is. There it is like a demon all weekend, a demon as big as a storm cloud sitting there all weekend, leaning down over her.

But Barclay is clear. Convinced her discernment is from God. Gifted is what he says. Gifted with discernment in such matters. Clearly the evil one is at work.

Another Home Fellowship. Sharing, praise reports. Twila talks about an all female vocal group she is in, that is being developed with tie-ins to clothing and accessory and perfume manufacturers and retailers, that is to sing material that is not indecent, that could appeal to Christians but not exclusively so. Three women in the group so far. One of the others is a Christian also. The three of them and their manager were interviewing a fourth awhile ago, a young woman in her twenties, and Twila is overwhelmed by a sense of pain around her head and shoulders and upper torso. And as she talks with the woman, she has a defeated feeling, a sense of oppression. Depression.

Later, after the candidate leaves, Twila and the others go out for a drink to discuss her, to determine whether she would be invited to join the group. Twila hesitatingly describes the sensations she has experienced, believing that this has to sound odd at best, but not knowing what else to do. She simply can't keep quiet about this. And she is told that the candidate has been abused by her husband for some time. That he has beaten her with some frequency and has in fact broken a few ribs at one point. Hospitalized. The woman left the man and is now in counseling.

Twila is smilingly at a loss as she speaks of it. At what God has given her. Wondering what to do with this gift. What to make of it. This charism. This difficult blessing.

Some places and times, maybe, Twila would be burned or drowned for these things. These days we enlarge the space in our minds for her, give God and her room to move around together. See what they must see, do what they must do. Become whatever astounding thing they must be.

It's at this point that Twila is no longer with us at church. What she says at the time is that her children want to go to church in their neighborhood. That they want to go to church with children they are likely to go to school with, might get together with after church. And so far as it goes, this is true.

But now, a year later, as she thinks about it, she thinks she also leaves our church because it's scary. The discernment thing. What is God telling her and about whom? She senses spiritual warfare in our church, and it's freaky. Being whirled about in something she doesn't quite get altogether and certainly cannot control. Just comes to a place spiritually where she needs to clear out. Transport herself out of the maelstrom. Out of the ambiguity and ambivalent emotions and conflicting allegiances. A nightmarishness maybe. And she settles out in a conservative church. A place where her spirit is given peace. Given some space for itself. Where it isn't jostled and battered by external forces. Where it is allowed to go its own way.

The church she ends up in is a different denomination. But this is nothing. Denominations are nothing. It is Jesus Twila and the rest of us think about, we all converse with. We leave the theologians to discuss things among themselves; we will pray to Jesus. We read the theologians for entertainment but pray for Love.

So now neither Twila nor Anne Marie nor Scotty attends our church but are regulars at the Home Fellowship. I miss them Sundays. I miss Twila's smile before us and her voice underpinning us, lifting us up as we sing.

There is unaccountable joy in song, and particularly when people with excellent voices can be heard above one's own. One sings with enthusiasm, but one enjoys it most when one's voice is lost in the extraordinary voices of the band and of those betters around one. With Twila's voice gone, the songs are less. We are less.

Susan's fortieth birthday dinner at Anne Marie's restaurant, Twila tells me she loses it last weekend with Travis. He's watching TV while she's digging in the garden, cleaning her house, preparing a meal, shopping, errands, controlling her children, reprimanding her dog, nailing up pictures, helping her children to study, paying the bills, *et cetera.* She has asked his help many times, and he has agreed but has done nothing she could recall. These were specific requests having to do with weeding or a front step that needed nailing or mowing or planting or affixing a mirror to a door or screwing a circular fan into the ceiling or cleaning the fireplace or taking out the garbage or cleaning out the garage or something like one or several of these.

For weeks. For months. She has been asking.

Oh, he works 60 to 80 hours a week. He's tired. It's understandable. But it has been going on forever. Forever. And it just can't go on anymore. How could it? Nothing is getting done. Or put correctly, something is getting done, but it isn't enough.

The children and house are hers alone and they are too much, too many. And she suddenly feels as though she cannot do it all, get it all done, like a woman whose only weapons are a broom and a bucket in a hundred year flood that rises from a nearby river—called, let's say, the Saint Johns River—a river that has been thoroughly filled by a once-in-a-century hurricane, which used to be just down her street, which is now rising into her yard and then rises into her house, inexorably, gradually but steadily, never deviating in its rising, in its enveloping, in its easing everything under its influence, in its submergence of what will be submerged, in its sending down river the things that will be dislodged and floated, in the dislocation of everything in its huge Old Testament rising.

She smiles as she tells me the story, as though she cannot quite, still, believe it, as though this really isn't her, and it really isn't him. As though they have found themselves in a story rather than in their proper and familiar lives, a story in which they find themselves playing parts that do not belong to them or suit them, parts that are ill fitting as the costumes in a civic theater are sometimes ill fitting because the revenues just aren't there.

"What should I do, Bill? I mean, you're a man. A husband. You've got that angle on things. What should I do different? Should I approach this thing differently, you know? I mean, I've tried suggestions. I've tried requests. I've tried joking about it. I've tried hiring people to do things, but he says he can do it, whatever it is. You know, the particular thing at the time. And besides, he says, it would cost too much money.

"I don't know. I'm just out of ideas, I guess. Do you have any? One?"

What I want to say is that I'm not the one to ask because Travis and I could be twins. What I want to say is that I have no idea. That I'm just as lazy as Travis is. That this is the way men are made. It's our job to sit on the couch and read or watch TV or nap or play golf or go out drinking with the guys or one of a legion of things that are useless and frivolous and silly. It's our job to leave the household and the children to our wives. Our job's somewhere else pushing paper or electrons, having meetings, telephoning, making decisions. Our job's bringing home a pay check. When we're home, our job is done. By definition. Except of course to cause our wives to smoke the drapes and drink their gin straight in big gulps from a shoe.

What I want to say is don't ask me because I personally have no idea.

But I have to say something. So why not say something fairly close to being useful? I try. What I do say is something about treating the house like a business. Like here's the problem. Let's put together a list of action items. Assign them. Determine due dates. Then have regular meetings in which everyone reports on progress. Old action items are retired as they are completed, new ones assigned. Treat it like a business, I suggest. Might like that better. Familiar machinery. Impersonal mostly. Just a get-it-done type of thing.

But I already think this might not work. It's business-like. Not home-like. Home is supposed to operate on different principles. What I'm going for is too much like the workplace. Too much like the dollar economics of the workplace rather than the affective economics of the home.

"Maybe that might work," she says, a puzzled look about her eyes and mouth, imagining this.

"I don't know," I say. "Try it. May be."

# Notes

**Lead Quotes**
"The books the Holy Spirit ... in every moment." Page 6.

Jean-Pierre de Caussade, *The Sacrament of the Present Moment*, Translated by Kitty Muggeridge, Harper & Row, Publishers, San Francisco, 1982, page 74.

**Barclay**
"There is one spirituality ... from death to life." Page 40.

Brennan Manning, *The Signature of Jesus*, Multnomah Books, Sisters, Oregon, 1996, pages 116-117.

**Ed**
"Glory be to God ... Praise Him." Page 78.

Gerard Manley Hopkins, "Pied Beauty," in *The New Oxford Book of English Verse*, Helen Gardner, editor, Oxford University Press, New York, 1997, page 787.

"The threefold terror … my hair stand up?"  Pages 78-79.

William Butler Yeats, "The Mother of God," in *Selected Poems and Four Plays of William Butler Yeats*, Fourth Edition, M.L. Rosenthal, editor, Scribner Paperback Poetry, 1996, page 140.

# About the Author

Bill Elkington was trained in writing at the University of Michigan and Syracuse University, receiving Master's and Doctor's degrees in English, with a concentration in creative writing. He has spent the last 23 years in the electronics and communications industries. He is currently working in the field of intellectual property management and licensing in Cedar Rapids, Iowa. He renewed his commitment to Christ three years ago and subsequently became involved in a church in Florida, where he participated in and then helped lead several Alpha courses. While there, he participated in a remarkable home fellowship. He and his wife, Pat, of 30 years have two children, both Christians. Praise God.

To order additional copies of

# taking note

Write to: orders@llumina.com

Printed in the United States
16606LVS00001B/493-516